Security Management

Ing. Jacques A. Cazemier

Dr. Ir. Paul L. Overbeek

Drs. Louk M.C. Peters

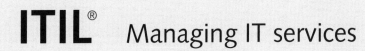

London: TSO

Published by TSO (The Stationery Office) and available from:

Online
www.tso.co.uk/bookshop

Mail, Telephone, Fax & E-mail
TSO
PO Box 29, Norwich, NR3 1GN
Telephone orders/General enquiries: 0870 600 5522
Fax orders: 0870 600 5533
E-mail: book.orders@tso.co.uk
Textphone 0870 240 3701

TSO Shops
123 Kingsway, London, WC2B 6PQ
020 7242 6393 Fax 020 7242 6394
68–69 Bull Street, Birmingham B4 6AD
0121 236 9696 Fax 0121 236 9699
9–21 Princess Street, Manchester M60 8AS
0161 834 7201 Fax 0161 833 0634
16 Arthur Street, Belfast BT1 4GD
028 9023 8451 Fax 028 9023 5401
18-19 High Street, Cardiff CF10 1PT
029 2039 5548 Fax 029 2038 4347
71 Lothian Road, Edinburgh EH3 9AZ
0870 606 5566 Fax 0870 606 5588

TSO Accredited Agents
(see Yellow Pages)

and through good booksellers

Published for the Office of Government Commerce under licence from the Controller of Her Majesty's Stationery Office.

First published 1999
Ninth Impression 2005

ISBN 0 11 330014 X

For further information regarding OGC products please contact:
OGC Help Desk, Rosebery Court, St Andrews Business Park, Norwich NR7 0HS
0845 000 4999

Printed in the United Kingdom for The Stationery Office
180006 c30 07/05

■ CONTENTS

ABOUT THE AUTHORS

Ing. Jacques Cazemier is the principal consultant on information security for Origin which is one of the leading IT service organisations.

Dr. Ir. Paul Overbeek is senior EDP Audit manager, working on information security and EDP – auditing for KPMG, one of the big four consultancy and accountancy firms.

Drs. Louk Peters is knowledge officer and strategic analyst for Pink Elephant, one of the founding organisations for ITIL.

ACKNOWLEDGEMENTS

The assistance of the following contributors to the development of this book is gratefully acknowledged:

Erwin de Bont MSc	Royal Netherlands Air Force
Peter Hoogendoorn	KPMG EDP Auditors
Ir. Hans Linschooten	Hewlett-Packard
D'Arcy McCallum	GE Capital IT Solutions
Colin Meadon	South Staffordshire Health Information Systems
Paul Peursum	Inter Access Interprom
Hannah Robertson	CAP Gemini
Frances Scarff	OGC
James E. Siminoski	GE Capital IT Solutions, Canada
Fred van Noord	Quint Wellington Redwood

FOREWORD

Organisations are increasingly dependent on electronic delivery of services to run their businesses and to meet customer needs. This means a requirement for high quality IT services, matched to business needs and user requirements as they evolve. OGC's IT Infrastructure Library (ITIL) provides a cohesive set of best practice, drawn from the public and private sectors internationally, supported by a comprehensive qualification scheme and accredited training organisations.

Bob Assirati
Executive Director, IT Directorate, OGC

MANAGEMENT SUMMARY

Information is one of the most important assets for business. Without it only a few processes are able to perform as intended. The sharing of information with other organisations, which enables quick and automated processing, increases that importance.

For information technology (IT), information is the core of its existence. Anything that threatens information or the processing of that information will directly endanger the performance of the organisation. Whether it concerns the confidentiality, accuracy, or timeliness of the information, the availability of processing functions or confidentiality, threats that form risks have to be countered by security. The aspects mentioned are structural for IT. That means that there are structural risks. Structural risks require structural security.

ITIL provides a foundation for the management of the IT Infrastructure. This book builds on that basis and explains how to organise and maintain the management of security of the IT infrastructure, from the IT manager's point of view.

The Service Level Agreement (SLA) defines the services agreed between customer and IT service provider. It contains a section on information security. In it, the required level of confidentiality, integrity and availability is defined. To accommodate this, the IT organisation that provides the IT services will have a corporate policy on how to deal with information security. For specific IT systems or IT subjects, an issue-specific policy may exist. As well as being active at the policy level, Security Management is also active at the tactical (e.g. implementation plans) and operational level. Based on the SLA, security measures need to be devised to meet the requirements. Starting from the SLA, Security Management enables and ensures that:

- measures are implemented and maintained to address changing circumstances like requirements, IT architecture elements, threats etc.
- security incidents are dealt with
- audit results show the adequacy of measures taken
- reports are produced to show the status of information security.

Maintenance is an important issue in Security Management since the IT world is changing continuously. Only a managed organisation with integrated feedback (like a closed loop system) is able to react accurately. Audit and evaluation are vital.

The ITIL Security Management process, as described in this book, takes existing ITIL processes as a starting point and adds Security Management activities to these processes. The ITIL Security Management process, although a separate process, is thus integrated as far as possible into the other processes. The following ITIL processes have the most important relationship with Security Management:

- Service Level Management
- Availability Management
- Performance and Capacity Management
- Business Continuity Planning
- Financial Management and Costing
- Configuration and Asset Management
- Incident Control/Help Desk

- Problem Management
- Change Management
- Release Management.

In order to aid in implementing and performing Security Management, best practice measures and guidelines are given in the last chapters and annexes of this book. The BSI Code of Practice for Information Security Management is used as reference.

▮ INTRODUCTION

1.1   What is Security Management

Questions to consider

What would you do if you came in the office to find disks labelled 'confidential' on the desk?

What would you do if you came in the office to find a PC was still powered up and logged on?

What would you do if you came in the office to find a batch of mail marked 'confidential' on the desk of a colleague who is on holiday?

Did you ever give your user ID and password to a colleague and worry about it being misused?

How well is the procedure organised and controlled for getting and storing keys that provide admission to various critical IT rooms, lockers, etc.?

Could any outside person just walk into your office building?

What would you do if your laptop was stolen during a business trip?

What if engineers of a subcontractor use laptops to run diagnostic software and introduce a virus?

Security Management is the process of managing a defined level of security on information and IT services. Included is managing the reaction to security incidents. The importance of information security has increased dramatically because of the move of open internal networks to customers and business partners; the move towards electronic commerce, the increasing use of public networks like Internet and Intranets. The wide spread use of information and information processing as well as the increasing dependency of process results on information requires structural and organised protection of information.

Security Management is more than locking server rooms or insisting on password discipline. Integrity aspects of information processing like timeliness or correctness require careful consideration of information flows and safeguards against incorrect values.

Information security incidents are those events that can cause damage to confidentiality, integrity or availability of information or information processing. They materialise as accidents or deliberate acts. Throughout this book the term 'security incident' is used to indicate such an event.

Security Management is a part of every manager's job. Management is responsible for taking appropriate measures to reduce the chances of failure to an acceptable level. Acceptable risks is the keyword. This requires that the subject of Security Management is taken seriously. Security Management has definite strategic, tactical and operational aspects. For example, separation of functions is one of the organisational measures to prevent misuse of information which can lead to fraud.

1.2   Purpose

This book helps organisations in Security Management in a practical, structured manner. It has elements of a workbook and is meant to be of practical assistance to the reader. This document is intended to support IT management. Like quality, information security is a management responsibility. Confidentiality, integrity and availability of services and information have to be assured. The required effort depends on the demands of the IT users. For example, in defence environments more emphasis is placed on confidentiality, while in finance the focus will be on integrity and in health care it could be on availability.

This book describes the best practices in Security Management. It is not essential to implement all of the guidance in this book. Different elements of the ITIL Security Management process may be used and adapted in different ways to meet the reader's specific situation. Common sense is essential when implementing Security Management.

1.3   Context

This book forms part of the IT Infrastructure Library. While it is of value to be read in isolation, its benefit to the organisation comes from the broader understanding and application of an integrated set of IT service management techniques.

Security Management is not an isolated process. It is always part of management, IT and business as a whole. The relationship between Security Management and the ITIL processes in the Service Support Set and the Service Delivery Set is therefore an important subject in this book. Furthermore, to use what is already available, standard ITIL processes are used to perform Security Management tasks wherever possible. These tasks in each ITIL process should take care of the security aspects in their specific area but the point of control of these tasks is centralised by the security management process.

Security Management is governed by a corporate policy. That policy is the corporate decision to spend time and money on the security of information and services. It provides the management with directions and guidelines. Sometimes a security policy is used to set out what is allowed and what is forbidden in use of IT systems. Within ITIL practices, this information is normally found in (annexes to) the Service Level Agreement (SLA).

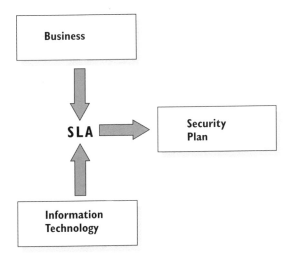

Figure 1.1: Service Level Agreement between business processes and IT processes

Figure 1.1 shows that both business processes and IT processes interact through the SLA. In the SLA, objectives for information security are defined. Security measures are stated based on the security requirements in the Service Level Requirements, which are derived from and formulated within the boundaries of the corporate policy on security. The Security Plan is the implementation plan based on the corporate policy on information security and the specific security requirements of the process.

> Almost all business processes require information and information processing. And in almost every case that information is crucial – without it the process will not produce its required result.
>
> It is therefore the business process which drives the specification of information security.

The first question relating to Security Management is: what security measures are needed? This may be determined with help of risk analyses. By using risk analysis an organisation gets formal and auditable means to define the security requirements. Risk analysis is important to decide which countermeasures to take against the risks involved. It should be performed structurally and also be embedded in the normal process for adopting changes to ensure that the measures taken are still adequate in spite of changing organisation, IT infrastructure or environment.

Security Management activities are found in almost every ITIL process because part of management is deciding about risks and dealing with them. Therefore this book is relevant to each and every ITIL process.

1.4 Scope

This book describes Security Management within the boundaries of ITIL. Important though they are, management of physical security or personal safety are not covered. Although certain aspects of this management appear to be identical, the measures and operations involved with these types of security do not fit within the scope of ITIL. However, an IT security incident may well involve many aspects of physical, personal and other areas of security within the same incident.

The technical details of devising and incorporating security measures are also beyond the scope of this book. Although crucial to the success of information security, its management merely uses the results of risk analysis. Therefore, risk analysis is outside the scope of this book. Risk analysis itself may be performed in many ways and is both a matter of specific business needs and of personal taste.

There are ITIL processes which cover facets of Security Management. For example, Availability Management and Business Continuity Planning are ITIL processes that in particular deal with some important aspects of Security Management. Although in this book we will refer to those processes, the reader is advised to read the relevant books themselves.

1.5   Target audience

This book is intended for all managers responsible for critical IT processes. This book is also relevant to business managers to help them to define the required security. It provides assistance in determining what aspects of security need to be included in the SLA.

The target audience therefore includes:

- IT Director
- IT Manager
- IT Services Manager
- IT Service Level Manager
- Risk and Security Manager
- Business Information Manager
- Business Managers
- Procurement Managers
- Supplier Managers
- Account Managers
- Auditors
- Consultants.

1.6   Structure of the document

After this brief introduction, Chapter 2 provides background information on information security and explains the basics of the information Security Management process. Chapter 3 describes the links with ITIL processes and the embedding of security relevant activities in the normal ITIL processes. Chapter 4 deals with the information security measures themselves. Chapter 5 presents some guidelines for implementing Security Management to help an organisation to translate theory into practice.

At the end of the book, several annexes give more information that will be helpful in implementing and performing Security Management:

- Annex A. Security Management with ITIL in relation to the Code of Practice for Information Security Management (BS7799)
- Annex B. Specimen security section in the SLA
- Annex C. Framework for drawing up a security plan
- Annex D. Literature
- Annex E. Glossary of terms.

1.7 New Terminology

This volume introduces the modern terminology which is being used throughout ITIL future publications. It also introduces the new model – see Figure 3.1 – which explains the links between the core parts of ITIL. The new terms are shown in Figure 1.2:

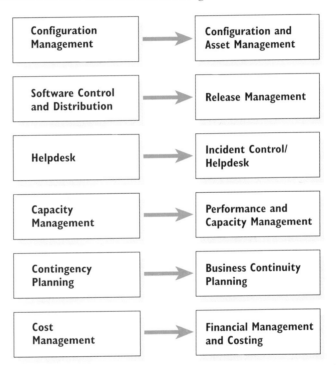

Figure 1.2: Modern ITIL terminology

2 FUNDAMENTALS OF INFORMATION SECURITY

2.1 Introduction

This section describes information security, first from a business perspective, and then from the perspective of the management of the IT infrastructure.

The pace of information technology (IT) developments is increasing. New application possibilities are also being created, especially through the integration of IT and telecommunications. However, changes in the technology and its use also necessitate changes in security requirements, so management of security becomes a necessity.

2.2 Information security from the business perspective

An organisation has formulated objectives. Business processes take place in an organisation in order to achieve these objectives. In executing these processes, the organisation becomes increasingly dependent on a well-functioning information supply. In other words organisations are increasingly dependent on IT services to meet their business needs. In this context, information security is not a goal in itself but a means of achieving the business objectives.

The way the information supply is organised depends on the type of organisation and the nature of the products or services it delivers in support of its business processes. The organisation collects data in order to make products or supply a service. The data is stored, processed and made available at the moment it is needed. Those people concerned have to be able to count on its integrity. And it is equally important to ensure that only those who are authorised to do so, can gain access to this information. By the time it is needed, confidentiality, integrity, and availability should no longer be open to discussion. An organisation must therefore organise the collection, storage, handling, processing and provision of data in such a way that these conditions are satisfied.

Information security exists to serve the interests of the business or organisation. Not all information and not all information services are equally important to the organisation. The level of information security has to be appropriate to the importance of the information. This 'tailored security' is achieved by finding a balance between the security measures and their associated costs on the one hand and, on the other, the value of the information and the risks in the processing environment. Security forms an important added value for an information system. After all, having the right security for an information system means that more tasks can be performed in an accountable and responsible manner.

2.2.1 Value of information

Information security is intended to safeguard information. *Security* is the means of achieving an acceptable level of residual risks. The *value* of the information has to be protected. This value is determined in terms of confidentiality, integrity and availability.

- *Confidentiality*: protecting sensitive information from unauthorised disclosure or intelligible interception
- *Integrity*: safeguarding the accuracy and completeness of information and software
- *Availability*: ensuring that information and vital IT services are available when required.

Some aspects that are derived from the above include *privacy* (the confidentiality and integrity of information traceable to a particular person), *anonymity* (the confidentiality of a user's identity) and *verifiability* (the possibility of verifying that information is being used properly and of demonstrating that the security measures are working properly).

The importance of having a proper information supply and also adequate information security, is twofold for an organisation:

- *Internal importance*: An organisation can only operate properly if it has access to confidential, accurate and complete information in good time. Information security has to be in line with this, ensuring that confidentiality, integrity and availability of information and information services is maintained.
- *External importance*: An organisation's processes supply products and services, which are made available in the market or the community, in order to achieve set objectives.

An inadequate information supply leads to imperfect products or services, thereby preventing the objectives from being fully achieved and threatening the continued existence of the organisation. Having adequate information security is an important precondition for an adequate information supply. Note that this applies to both the public and private sectors.

Besides the flow of results (products and services), countless information streams also flow from the environment to the organisation, internally through the organisation, and from the organisation to the environment. If these streams suddenly dry up, the organisation is no longer capable of operating properly. Information is a means of production on which organisations have become increasingly reliant over the years.

The degree to which the business processes depend on the information supply has to be specified in quality requirements for the information supply. In that sense, information security must therefore form an integral part of an organisation's overall quality management and quality assurance procedures. The utilisation goal of information in an organisation depends very much on the process in which the information is used. The requirements set for the information supply should therefore largely come from the people who manage the processes.

2.2.2   Security measures

An important issue in Security Management is the degree to which an organisation's management is willing to make a specific commitment to protecting the information, by making resources available (people, time, money). This commitment should be made on the basis of the available resources and the required level of information security. After all, not all information and information services are equally important to the organisation. It is the value of the information that has to be protected. Security measures can limit the risks and vulnerability.

Security measures make it possible to reduce or eliminate the risks associated with information and IT. The starting point and by far the most important point is to have a good security *organisation*, with clear responsibilities and tasks, guidelines, reporting procedures and measures that are properly matched to the needs of the business and the IT. *Physical* security measures, such as the physical separation of the computer room, are well understood. *Technical* security measures provide security in a computer system or network. This is, for example, the security offered by the operating system for the segregation of users. *Procedural* security measures describe how the staff are required to act in particular cases. For example, there must be procedures that describe who has access to the computer area and when, or procedures that describe when an 'account' expires and what has to be done with the information that is still available.

Security measures add value only when used harmoniously. The security organisation has to manage and maintain a proper balance.

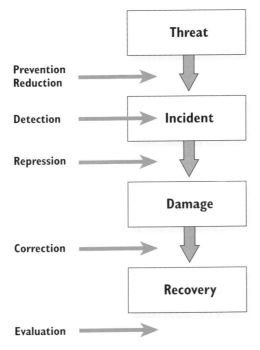

Figure 2.1: From threat to recovery

Security measures can be used in a specific stage in the prevention and handling of security incidents, see Figure 2.1. Security incidents are not solely caused by technical threats – statistics show that, for example, the large majority stem from human errors (intended or not) or procedural errors, and often have implications in other fields such as safety, legal or health.

The following stages can be identified. At the start there is a risk that a threat will materialise. A threat can be anything that disrupts the business process or has negative impact on the business results. When a threat materialises, we speak of a security incident. This security incident may result in damage (to information or to assets) that has to be repaired or otherwise corrected.

Suitable measures can be selected for each of these stages. The choice of measures will depend on the importance attached to the information.

Preventive security measures are used to prevent a security incident from occurring. The best known example of preventive measures is the allocation of access rights to a limited group of authorised people. The further requirements associated with this measure include the control of access rights (granting, maintenance and withdrawal of rights), authorisation (identifying who is allowed access to which information and using which tools), identification and authentication (confirming who is seeking access), access control (ensuring that only authorised personnel can gain access).

Further measures can be taken in advance to minimise any possible damage that may occur. These are '*reductive*' measures. Familiar examples of reduction measures are making regular backups and the development, testing and maintenance of contingency plans.

If a security incident occurs, it is important to discover it as soon as possible: *detection*. A familiar example of this is monitoring, linked to an alert procedure. Another example is virus checking software.

Repressive measures are then used to counteract any continuation or repetition of the security incident. For example, an account or network address is temporarily blocked after numerous failed attempts to log on or the retention of a card when multiple attempts are made with a wrong PIN number.

The damage is repaired as far as possible using *corrective* measures. For example, corrective measures include restoring the backup, or returning to a previous stable situation (roll back, back out). Fallback can also been seen as a corrective measure.

In the case of serious security incidents, an *evaluation* is necessary in due course, to determine what went wrong, what caused it and how it can be prevented in the future. However, this process should not be limited to serious security incidents. All breaches of security need to be studied in order to gain a full picture of the effectiveness of the security measures as a whole. A reporting procedure for security incidents is required to be able to evaluate the effectiveness and efficiency of the present security measures based on an insight into *all* security incidents. This is facilitated by the maintenance of log files and audit files, and of course, the records of the ITIL Incident Control/Help Desk function, which are discussed later in more detail.

2.2.3 The business perspective: how can we manage information security

The starting point is the proper *organisation* of information security, i.e. responsibilities, powers and duties are clearly specified in reducing levels of abstraction:

- policy and/or codes of conduct (which *objectives* we are aiming for)
- processes (*what* has to happen to achieve those objectives)
- procedures (*who* does what and *when*)
- work instructions (*how* do we specifically do that and when and where).

Information and information processing are crucial to support business processes. Nowadays IT not only supports the business but can even act as a promoter for generating more business (i.e. the opportunities presented by the Internet). Since all business has to deal with a lot of changes in the business and legal changes (country dependent), this could have a big impact on IT security requirements. Information security is an integral part of all business processes. With the right security, the business objectives are supported and their achievement is assured, even when internal or external negative influences occur or if the IT fails.

Maintaining information security is an iterative process. All the factors that influence its results (and therefore have to be acted upon) are seen as inputs. There are internal and external influences that have their effect on information security. The internal influences are caused by decisions within the organisation. External influences are influences that come from the environment in which the business processes take place. This makes Security Management a challenge.

Examples of changes in input which require adaptation of the process are:

- changes in tasks or the importance of tasks
- physical alterations, e.g. after moving premises

- environmental alterations
- changes in assessment of the IT used
- changes in business demands
- changes in legal demands
- changes in hardware and/or software
- changes in business demands
- changes in legal requirements
- changes in threats
- the introduction of new technology.

The result should be that, seen from a business perspective, the Security Management process provides a large degree of confidence that a level of confidentiality, integrity and availability has been achieved, which is sufficient for the business' purposes, and sufficient for the organisation's (business) partners.

The developments in information security began in the early 1970s. The developments in information security took place independently of developments in IT management. Whether this was a good thing or not is no longer relevant. Today, it is generally recognised that management and security are inseparable twins. The model below shows the management model for information security, from a business' perspective.

Figure 2.2: Information Security model

Figure 2.2 represents the complete information security process during all the phases of its cycle, from implementation to maintenance.

Top management support is a must for information security. A structured approach to information security invariably starts with the top management decision to 'do it', since it involves investments both in infrastructure and in organisation. The decision is recorded in the information security policy, which forms the mandatory management guidelines on, among other things, the organisation, establishing the management framework, responsibilities, scope and depth.

Risk analyses may be performed to define the security needs from a business perspective as well as from a technical perspective. These analyses clarify the current status and quality of information security (the current situation) as well as the security measures that are to be implemented (the desired situation). The required situation is described in a security plan. Planning is required to move from the current to the desired situation. After implementation, operation of the measures forms part of normal day-to-day operations. Management uses the management framework to review the effectiveness and efficiency of the implementation of the security measures. These reviews also provide the necessary feedback to either improve the implementation or improve the plan. This input is used in the periodic (yearly) security improvement plans. Of course, the results of the audits also provide input to adapt the policy, or to improve the 'tool kit' for Security Management, including, for example, the risk analysis tools.

This book does not prescribe any method of risk analysis, such as the CCTA Risk Analysis and Management Methodology (CRAM). Although risk analysis helps in identifying risks and the selection of measures, it should only be applied where and when needed. Management in general is concerned about money as in cost and revenue. In information security measures, these aspects are to be treated seriously in order to avoid the image of cost-only activity. Therefore the outcome of a risk analysis should take the form of a balance, in which both risks and measures are (at least qualitatively) balanced between their 'costs' and their 'revenues'.

When a risk analysis is carried out professionally, management will obtain a positive feeling about information security and is able to make decisions at the management level without the need to understand technical details.

2.2.4 Business benefits

Information security is about assurance. A manager should feel 'in control'. Proper information security assures the continuity of the business, and the achievement of business' goals.

To secure the IT infrastructure costs money (in terms of resources, maintenance and control). Not to secure the IT infrastructure also costs money (in terms of costs of lost production, replacement costs of stolen or damaged data/equipment, compensation payments for unachieved contractual obligations). Estimating the costs requires business knowledge in order to produce financial values. It is even more important to estimate losses because of political embarrassment, adverse publicity, loss of customer confidence.

Effective Security Management depends on accurate risk analysis so that knowledge of the impact of risks and the costs of avoidance is understood. Without it, the tendency is either to ignore risks in the hope that they never happen, or expend disproportionate amounts of time and money on avoiding risks of minor potential impact. Risks are an inevitable feature of life, but only manageable risks should be permitted. Security management is concerned with those activities that are required to *maintain* the risks at manageable proportions, e.g. evaluation of effectiveness of measures, registration and trend analysis of security incidents.

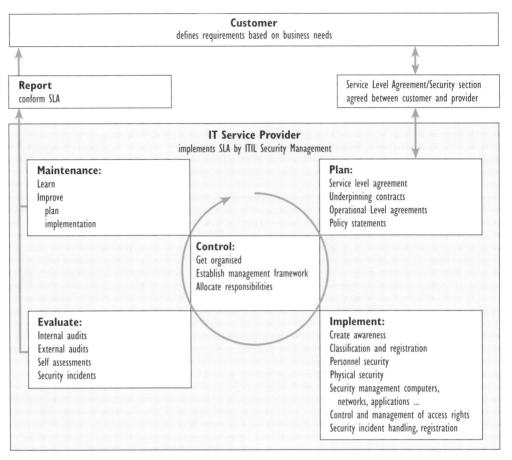

Figure 2.3: The IT Security Management process

2.3 Information security from the IT management perspective

For the IT service provider, either being an in-house computing department or an outsourced IT provider, the policies and the risk analysis from Figure 2.2 (looking from a business perspective) are the responsibility of the customer's organisation. The demands that result from these analyses are input into the security plans. These plans may concern a modest variety of subjects, ranging from, for example, physical security of the buildings, personnel security, plans for financial security. For IT Security Management, these plans define the security demands for IT. These are generally called the security service level requirements, and are reflected in the SLA between the customer (the business) and the IT service organisation (the IT service provider). It is the responsibility of the service provider to detail these generic security service level requirements in specific security measures per system and/or per organisational unit within the IT service provider's organisation. The service provider may also use risk analysis to assess the IT risks.

2.3.1 The IT Security Management process

For Security Management within the IT environment, the activities in the lower part of the model in Figure 2.2 are the most relevant (planning, operational measures, evaluation and audit), but only as far as these activities are concerned with the management of IT. The upper part and other activities (not concerning IT) should be in place! Annex A addresses exactly these activities, since the authors felt it would not be right to leave these subjects out just because they do not fit neatly in the management of IT.

Figure 2.3 focuses on the Figure 2.2 activities that are relevant to the IT service provider. This figure gives an overview of the management process for the security of IT and the information in the IT environment (called the IT Security Management process). Note:

- that Figure 2.3 only considers the process of managing the SLA between the customer and a single service provider. Situations may arise where multiple SLAs exist, sometimes with more than one service provider, and the user needs to examine to what extent this will create additional security implications and whether there is a need for inter-communication between the various service providers, possibly managed by a lead service provider or separately by the user

- that this process, like any other process, involves a closed loop.

Input for this process is the security section of the Service Level Agreement, which is the translation of the customer's business needs into the specifications of the security services offered by the IT service provider. The section on security in the SLA deals with the demands for information security and the way in which these requirements are planned and implemented. The figure shows the full route from a customer's *requirements* to the IT service provider, and back, in the form of result *reports* to the customer. Note that there is no principal difference between internal and external customers or between internal and external IT service providers. An in-house IT service provider should provide just as professional a service as an outsourced IT service provider.

Information security has to be *controlled*, *planned*, *implemented*, *evaluated* and *maintained*. Regular status *reporting* to the customer closes the loop. The activities within IT Security Management are defined on the basis of this overview.

The IT Security Management process deals with information security from the perspective of IT management. Therefore, IT Security Management manages all the measures that provide the required confidence in the IT facilities.

Confidence and reliability, sufficient for the customer's needs, result from the IT Security Management process. This process is further subdivided into six activities (see Figure 2.3).

2.3.1.1 Control

The Control activity organises and directs the IT Security Management process itself. This includes the organisation of the management framework for information security. The management framework contains the way the security plans are established, the process through which these are implemented, the way in which the implementation is evaluated, the process through which the results of these evaluations are used for the maintenance of security plans and the implementation thereof, and, finally, the reporting structure to the customer.

The Control activity defines the (sub) processes, functions, roles, allocation of responsibilities within the sub-processes, the organisation structure between these and the reporting structure/line of command.

The Control activity is fully aligned with the control activities within the other IT management processes. The process owner for IT Security Management, called the Security Manager, is a peer to his fellow process managers. Note that, depending on the organisation, the Security Manager can be a role or a function.

2.3.1.2   Plan

The Plan activity includes the way the security section of the SLA is established as well as the underpinning contracts. The generic security requirements in the SLA are refined in Operational Level Agreements (OLAs). OLAs are also known as 'back-to-back' agreements. They define support requirements internally (e.g., print server availability, network up-time). With respect to Security Management, these OLAs can be seen as the more detailed security plans for the organisational units of the IT service provider as well as the security handbook plans for the IT platforms.

The Plan activity may also use policy statements for the IT service provider itself (not to be confused by the policies of the customer). A policy statement could be: "every user has to be identified uniquely" or, "a basic set of security measures is offered to all customers and is always maintained".

The Plan activity within the Security Management process is aligned with the Service Level Management process in general. The Service Level Manager is leading in this effort.

The Operational Level Agreements for information security (the detailed security plans) follow the normal Change Management process. The Security Manager is responsible for providing the input. But the Change Manager is responsible for the Change Management process itself.

2.3.1.3   Implement

The Implement activity implements a whole range of measures as defined in the plans. In section 4 this range of activities is discussed in detail. To summarise some of the most important points:

- Maintaining awareness – Information security works because of discipline, and only when supported by clear documentation and procedures. In order to achieve effectiveness, motivation is absolutely necessary. The degree of effort required for informing and educating employees depends on the national and organisational culture. However, making security work always involves an investment.

- Security incident handling – The handling of security incidents has to be dealt with appropriately. Front doors that have been forced open cannot be left till another day. A rapid reaction is especially required when the consequences of security incidents cross organisational boundaries. Co-ordination with neighbouring organisations may be essential to locate the cause and origin of the incident.

- Security incident registration – is part of security incident control. Part of incident control is knowing whether similar incidents have occurred in the past and what solutions were used at the time. Security incident registration is also used to determine which part of the organisation experiences more security incidents (of a certain type) than others. This will be an indication that certain measures have to be enforced more rigorously or that different types of measures are in order. Security incident registration and handling, or, for short, security incident control, is part of the incident control process.

Again, any changes in the infrastructure take place through the Change Management process.

2.3.1.4 Evaluate

Blindly trusting security measures installed long ago will create an atmosphere of phantom security. Independent evaluation enables other parts of the organisation or third parties to have added confidence in the security measures. Evaluation results will also be used to maintain the measures taken. It might be necessary to update measures or to change measures for more effectiveness.

Evaluation is indispensable to close the loop of the Security Management system. It concerns the status and effectiveness of measures taken, it also concerns standards and policy. Evaluating results will provide feedback on the measures in operation. It even may indicate the need for a review of the measures. When this review results in a need for change, a Request for Change (RFC) will be submitted to the Change Management process.

Three types of evaluation are recognised:

- Internal audits (reviews performed by internal Electronic Data Processing (EDP) auditors)

- External audits (performed by external independent EDP auditors)
- Self assessments (performed within the line-organisation itself).

Furthermore, evaluation takes place based on the reported security incidents. These security incidents are passed to the Problem Management process for aggregation and trend analysis.

Evaluation, and in particular the information about the effectiveness of the measures provides the feedback that creates a closed-loop control system. Such a system is able to maintain and improve itself. Such a system is needed to be 'in control'.

2.3.1.5 Maintenance

Security measures have to be kept up to date, as the threats and the infrastructure, organisation and processes are changing constantly. Part of the maintenance effort has to be devoted to security handbooks. The books contain detailed descriptions of the measures and how to use them properly. The security handbooks have to be kept up to date, distributed and be readily available.

The maintenance of security measures is based on the results of the periodic reviews, insight into the changing risk picture, and, of course, changes in the input material (the security section in the SLA). The latter changes can also be made on the basis of new customer requirements. Another way of maintaining security measures is through the control of changes in the infrastructure as described above.

2.3.1.6 Report

Reporting is an activity in itself, although it is largely dependent on the results from other actions. Reporting takes place, for example, to support the control activities or simply because this was agreed upon in the SLA (relation with the Service Level Management process).

One of the major reasons information security has been neglected for so long is the absence of historical records, i.e. historical records of the mishaps in the individual organisation. Generally no one has any idea of what kinds of security incidents have troubled the organisation in the past. Aspects such as ignorance and the mistaken idea of not exposing the dirty linen are the most common reasons for this. There are many advantages of having a well documented security incident database. It enables a trend analysis to be made for certain types of security incidents or parts of the organisation, proves the necessity of certain measures, and provides the arguments necessary for demonstrating that specific measures are required.

There is no frame of reference for management to defend the investments made in security. Risk analysis may help in some cases, but, still, investments in security can seldom be based on hard figures. And, if they can, probably something went very wrong in the past. An investment plan will most likely be based on qualitative aspects: good housekeeping, good enough to avoid public embarrassment, acceptable risk, acceptable to our customers, conform to good market principles, conform to legal standards.

Reporting is important. Senior management of the customer has to be aware of the efficiency of the resources spent on security measures and the effectiveness of the measures. Not only the status of implementation, but also the impact of the measures has to be reported. Security incident handling can form a starting point for impact reports.

2.4   Relationship to other IT management processes

From the above, it must be clear that there are strong relationships between the activities of the IT Security Management process, and those in the other IT management processes. These relationships are enforced through the Control activity itself, and, as a matter of fact, also by the Control activities of the other IT processes. Figure 2.4 shows these relationships. The most important relationships have already been mentioned. When the activities are described in Chapter 4, these relationships are highlighted.

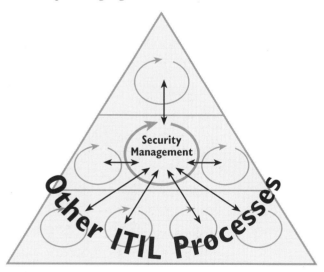

Figure 2.4: Relationships between Security Management and other processes

In the next chapter, the relationships are shown between IT Security Management in the ITIL context, and the other IT management processes as defined within ITIL.

3 ITIL AND SECURITY MANAGEMENT

The preceding chapter described the Security Management process in general terms. This chapter places that process within the context of ITIL and describes the most important processes in ITIL. In view of the multifaceted character of information security, we shall see that attention has to be paid to information security in many ITIL processes.

3.1 ITIL

ITIL describes the processes that are executed as part of the management of IT. These processes are combined in nine sets. *Security Management* is one of the ITIL processes. The *Security Management process* has important relationships with other processes, of which the most important, grouped into two sets, are described in this chapter.

ITIL is concerned with best *practice* in the management and exploitation of the IT infrastructure. ITIL has arisen from practical experience and this makes ITIL a recognisable and practice-based approach. Practice has also shown that using ITIL increases the quality of the IT service.

ITIL focuses on managing an existing working environment, and managing changes in that environment. ITIL is not specifically concerned with system development. Nor is ITIL concerned with the strategic and tactical processes required for developing the IT architecture and infrastructure. Also, ITIL does not specifically focus on corporate policy.

ITIL is not a cookbook with standard recipes that can be used blindly in every organisation. As an ITIL user and reader of this book, you will have to pick out the best ITIL practices for your needs. Also the ITIL implementation must be tailored to fit the IT service provider.

ITIL is concerned with the management and exploitation of the IT infrastructure. In ITIL, the IT infrastructure means software, applications, hardware, documentation, procedures and systems. ITIL is not primarily concerned with individual components, such as files, queues, data or messages. Nor is ITIL concerned with personnel matters, except for employees in their role as manager responsible for an ITIL process. The environment and the physical aspects are also largely beyond the scope of ITIL.

Clearly, these subjects have an effect on security. Annex A therefore contains a summary of advice concerned with what the *best practice* is for these subjects that are beyond the scope of ITIL.

3.1.1 Goals and placement of Security Management within ITIL

The model at Figure 3.1 describes the relationship between Security and the ITIL Core set. Every aspect of IT Service Management has Security Management considerations. There is a specific relationship with Availability Management – one of the prime aspects of security is Availability – and through this Business Continuity, but this should not be allowed to detract from its importance throughout the Service Management scenario.

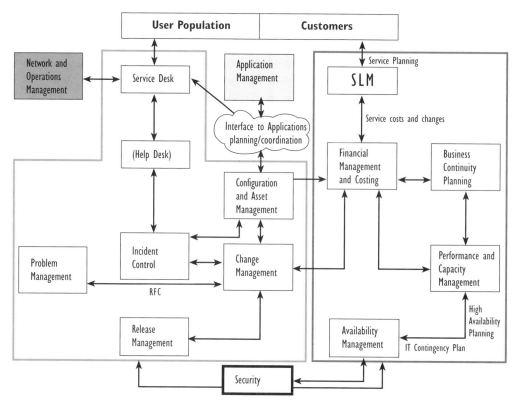

Figure 3.1: The ITIL Process Model

ITIL assumes an entirely process-based approach to management. Figure 3.2 shows the 'model'. Each ITIL process exists for a particular purpose (goal). The purpose is achieved through carrying out a set of activities. The inputs for this process are the specific demands regarding the process goals. The output of the process is the reporting about the quality with which these demands are fulfilled. The connection to the other processes is indicated in the 'relationship' box.

Figure 3.2: Process-based approach

The model for the Security Management process is given shape as follows:

The goal of the Security Management process is two-fold:

- First to meet the *external* security requirements. These result from the security requirements in the various SLAs. These external requirements for security also stem from contracts, legislation and any imposed security policy.

- Second to meet the *internal* security requirements. This is required to assure the IT service provider's own continuity. It is also necessary to simplify the Service Level Management for information security. After all, managing a large number of different

SLAs is much more complex than managing a small number. Therefore, for instance, a certain basic level of security (the so-called standard security baseline) needs to be established.

The *input* side of the process is formed by the SLAs and the specified security requirements they contain, possibly supplemented with policy documents.

The *output* provides reporting information concerning the fulfilment of the SLAs, therefore including reports on any non-conformities.

The SLA defines the services agreed upon between customer and IT service provider. Note that there is no principal difference between internal customers and external customers, nor between internal or external IT service providers. In all cases agreements should be made and understood by all parties to enable a professional management of IT services.

There are *relationships* between the Security Management process and most of the other ITIL processes. In order to describe these relationships, the layered structure of ITIL is presented.

Figure 3.3: Three layers in ITIL

The triangle in Figure 3.3 shows the three layers that can be thought of as a structure for ITIL. Each layer represents a level of abstraction. The processes are grouped according to these layers.

The top layer outlines the management strategy. The processes for this strategic layer are collected in the Manager's set. For information security, this set is particularly important with regard to the organisation of information security activities of the IT service provider. This set is particularly important if a specific security policy for the IT service provider has been defined.

The middle layer shows the tactical processes, grouped in the Service Delivery set. This is where the SLAs are drawn up and the service is provided in accordance with these agreements. Co-ordination with the customer is important when defining the security requirements laid down in the SLAs and for the provision of the service in accordance with these agreed security measures. The Security Management process is related to most of the other processes in this set, including:

- Service Level Management
- Availability Management
- Performance and Capacity Management, which covers:
  - Workload management
  - Performance management
  - Resource management
  - Demand management
  - Application sizing
  - Modeling

- Business Continuity Planning
- Financial Management and Costing.

Finally, there is the operational layer. The processes in this layer are grouped in the Service Support set. These are the beneficial processes for service delivery. The processes in the Service Support set assure the actual operational management of the IT resources themselves. The Security Management process depends very much on the processes in this set because these are beneficial for Security Management. Security Management is therefore related to practically all the processes in this set, these being:

- Configuration and Asset Management
- Incident Control/Help Desk
- Problem Management
- Change Management
- Release Management.

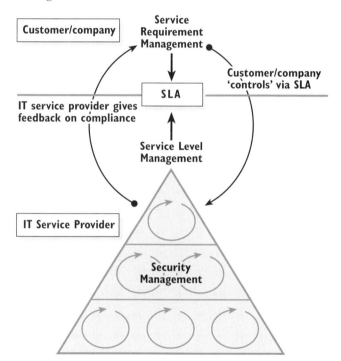

Figure 3.4: Related processes

ITIL therefore works on the basis of related processes, as is indicated in Figure 3.4. The control information for Service Level Management consists of the SLA, in which the agreements with the customer are specified. Reporting information is used to account for the performance of the IT service provider vis-à-vis the agreements in the SLA.

Service Level Management is based on the ITIL processes in the Service Delivery set. These have a mutual relationship and are in turn based on the processes in the Service Support set. These processes are also mutually related. Each process has an 'owner', being the process manager, who is responsible for the control of the process. The processes run in a cycle: plan—implement—evaluate—maintain as shown in Figure 2.3. A number of these related processes can collectively be seen as a 'larger' process. For example, in this figure all the ITIL processes together form the IT management process.

3.2   The security section in the Service Level Agreement

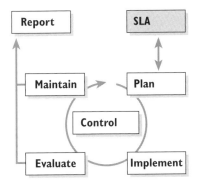

In order to explain how ITIL is used for information security, a clarification is first provided of how the security section in the SLA arises. Then, the processes in the Service Support set and those in the Service delivery set are discussed.

Figure 3.5 shows how the security section arises in the SLA.

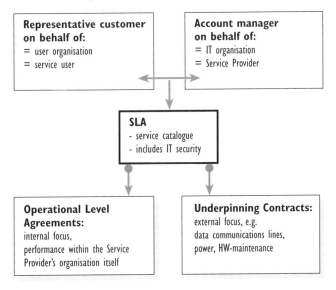

Figure 3.5: The SLA environment

A good way to start is to have an (independent) analysis carried out in which each business process is analysed for its requirements regarding confidentiality, integrity and availability (or continuity). The results are the *Service Level Requirements* for security. Although this is the responsibility of the 'owner' of a business process, IT management may assist in formulating these security requirements.

The representative of the customer (e.g. the business process owner) postulates the Service Level Requirements. These are compared with the IT service provider's *Service Catalogue*. The Service Catalogue also shows the security measures that are always provided: the basic level of security often called the *security baseline*. The customer may set additional requirements that exceed the security baseline as offered in the Service Catalogue. This may result in additional costs.

The customer and the Service Level Manager jointly determine the balance between the Service Level Requirements and the Service Catalogue.

In combination with the SLA there are other aspects to consider.

The first is that part of the services are dependent on third parties like the companies providing electrical power or data communication services. The IT service provider is often unable to take full responsibility for these services. For example, providers of telecommunication give no guarantee of the availability of leased lines. The IT service provider therefore agrees with his customer about which arrangements the provider will make with his telecom providers.

These agreements are known as the *Underpinning Contracts* (UCs). They consist of all the agreements for which the IT service provider is unable to take full responsibility, generally because he has no influence over the fulfilment of the agreements.

The second aspect to consider are the *Operational Level Agreements* (OLAs). These concern the activities (or detailed services) that have to be carried out within the IT service provider's organisation to offer the required services. These agreements are for use within the organisation of the IT service provider itself. It is important for the IT service provider to allocate internal responsibility for these agreements (see Annex C). The Service Catalogue provides a general description of the services. The Operational Level Agreements are a 'drill down' of these general descriptions into the services (*Service Delivery*) and the individual components – see the *Configuration Items* under Configuration and Asset Management – as well as the way in which the agreements about service levels are guaranteed internally.

> **Example**
>
> The Service Catalogue refers, for instance, to 'management of access rights per user, per person'. In the Operational Level Agreements, this is then regulated for the department within the organisation of the IT service provider that supplies the UNIX services, for VMS, for NT, for Oracle, and so forth.

When drawing up the SLA, it is also important for security reasons to agree on measurable Key Performance Indicators (or KPI) and performance criteria. KPI are the measurable quantities; the performance criteria are the achievable levels of the measurable quantities. However, for practical reasons the definition of the required measures for information security are often stated in the SLA's security section.

The SLA contains agreements about the way in which *performance* will be measured. In any case, it is necessary for the user organisation (the customer) to be provided with reporting information from and about the IT service provider.

Annex B includes an example of the composition of the SLA's security section.

3.3 The Service Support set and Security Management

The processes in the Service Support set are concerned entirely with managing the IT resources themselves. The processes in this set are recapped in this section, along with the way in which they support the Security Management process. The following processes are discussed:

- Configuration and Asset Management
- Incident Control/Help Desk
- Problem Management

- Change Management
- Release Management.

3.3.1 Configuration and Asset Management

A prerequisite for proper IT management is that the process for Configuration and Asset Management is set up properly. Configuration and Asset Management is the process that ensures that you know what is available to the organisation in terms of IT infrastructure, what its status is, and which relationships exist between the various components of the infrastructure (i.e. the relationships between the CIs, see below). In short, whether the inventory of the IT infrastructure is known. Configuration and Asset Management also ensures that changes in the IT infrastructure are only made in an accountable manner. Each change must be recorded in Configuration and Asset Management. Configuration and Asset Management forms, as such, the basis of IT management.

This process is intended to provide control over all the components of the IT infrastructure and the related procedures and documentation, by supporting the other processes, in order to provide high-quality services at a justifiable cost, within the context of ever-changing user requirements.

When Configuration and Asset Management is properly organised, it becomes clear which configuration items make up the IT infrastructure being managed, who is responsible for which item, where the items are, what the status is and what relationship(s) exist between the configuration items. Configuration and Asset Management provides information on the composition of the IT infrastructure and is responsible for correctly registering authorised parts of the IT infrastructure. Moreover, Configuration and Asset Management verifies whether the registration still correctly reflects the situation in reality. This method avoids having to work with unauthorised components that do not fulfil the security requirements.

There are two central concepts: a *Configuration Item* (CI) is the smallest unit that is managed individually. The overview of all the CIs also forms the overview of the total IT infrastructure. This overview is called the *Configuration and Asset Management Database* (CMDB). Possible configuration items in ITIL include software (applications), hardware, documentation and procedures.

3.3.1.1 Security Management and Configuration and Asset Management

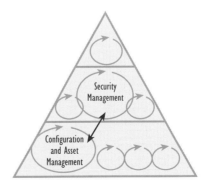

Each configuration item has a unique identification number. Records are also kept of each CI's attributes, the status, and the possible relationships to other CIs. In terms of information security, one aspect of Configuration and Asset Management which is especially important is the classifying of a CI. The classification links the CI to a particular set of security measures or a procedure.

A CI classification is an indication of the level of confidentiality, integrity and/or availability required for the CI. This classification is derived from the security requirements in the SLA. The customer of the IT service provider (usually a business process owner) determines the classification because that is the only person who can determine how important information or systems are for his business processes. The customer determines the classification on the basis of an analysis of the dependency of the business processes on the information systems and on the information itself. It is then up to the IT service provider to permanently link this classification to the right CIs. The IT service provider must also implement an individual package of security measures for each level of classification. The package of measures can be summarised in a procedure. Such a procedure may, for example, read: "procedure for handling data carriers with data classified as private". It is a good custom for a record to be entered in the SLA of which package of security measures has to be implemented for which level of classification.

A classification system must always be tailored to the needs of the customer's organisation. A few examples are provided below.

Confidentiality:

- High = Personal data as defined under the Data Protection Act (privacy related), medical records, strategic information
- Medium = Internal, must not go outside the company
- Low = External, everything that would be allowed to go outside the company.

Integrity:

- High = Financial transactions, software, personal data
- Medium = Measurement data, name & address data
- Low = No requirements.

Availability:

- High = 24 hours per day, 99.5%
- Medium = from 07.00 to 19.00, 99%
- Low = no guarantees required.

A few other recognised examples of confidentiality:

- Official: Secret, Confidential, Restricted, Unclassified
- NATO: Cosmic Top Secret, NATO Secret, NATO Confidential, NATO Restricted, NATO Unclassified.

Finally, an example from a government department is shown in Table 3.1.

Table 3.1: Example of classification system

	Valuation			
Security requirement	*No criterion* Security is not really necessary	*Advisable* A certain degree of security is appreciated	*Important* Security is absolutely necessary in view of the interests	*Essential* Security is a primary criterion
Confidentiality	*Public* The information may be published/made public	*Protected* Data only to be seen by particular group	*Crucial* Data only accessible to those directly involved	*Mandatory* Business interests would be severely damaged if accessed by unauthorised parties
Integrity	*Passive* No extra integrity protection required	*Active* Business process tolerates some errors	*Detectable* A very small number of errors is permitted	*Essential* Business process demands error-free information
Availability	*Unnecessary* No guarantees required	*Necessary* Occasional downtime is acceptable	*Important* Hardly any downtime during opening times	*Essential* Only out of operation in extremely exceptional circumstances

These examples show up to four levels of classification for confidentiality, integrity and availability. The more levels a classification system has, the more difficult it is to maintain. Therefore it is advisable to keep the number of levels as low as possible for your (and your customer's) needs.

In the most simple classification system, each security characteristic is designated simply as 'basic level' (to be linked to the set of standard measures of the *baseline*) or as additional requirements (to be linked to a more stringent set of measures).

An example of a simple classification system is:

- the baseline always applies
- additional requirements apply to confidentiality, if:
  - the information is of a strategic nature
  - the information is specially marked: 'medical', 'private & confidential', 'personal'
- additional requirements apply to integrity and availability, if:
  - the information and the systems are employed for uses of a strategic, mission or safety-critical nature.

To minimise the management overhead, it is advisable to use one classification system, even when an IT service provider has more than one customer.

To summarise: classification is a key concept. The CMDB contains the classification of each CI. The classification links the CI to a set of security measures that relates to the classification, or a procedure. Classification links a CI to specific activities, laid down as a procedure (handling instructions) in the documentation (handbooks, *implementation guidelines*). The procedure will often state that some type of record or reporting is required on implementation.

3.3.2   Incident Control/Help Desk

Incident Control/Help Desk is a single liaison point of contact within the organisation for end-users of services. This functional group is often referred to as a service desk and its core process is normally incident management. The main objective of this function is continuity in the service provided to the customers. This also means that users have to accept the Incident Control/Help Desk as the only source of help which in turn requires good access to the Incident Control/Help Desk. Providing continuity is the most important goal of incident management. The user has to be able to carry on working: if the user is satisfied with the solution, the incident can be closed from the ITIL point of view, even if the solution is simply 'press Ctrl-Alt-Del'. This process is concerned with the speed at which the solution to an incident is provided, and not with the quality of the solution, which is the domain of Problem Management (see 3.3.3).

The activities of the incident management process are the administration, monitoring and management of incidents (*incident control*). Incident Control/Help Desk is the central point where *all* incidents are registered and monitored and acts as a single source of help for all incident reports and first-line help. The Incident Control/Help Desk is the 'owner' of all the incidents.

The Incident Control/Help Desk records incidents and ensures that they are dealt with as quickly as possible. The Incident Control/Help Desk also has the possibility of escalation, if there is a likelihood of an incident not being solved in good time. This naturally also applies to incidents that concern security.

The Incident Control/Help Desk's input largely consists of reports from users. Incidents are categorised and for each category a procedure is defined that prescribes the activities that have to be carried out by the Incident Control/Help Desk. Accurate categorisation is essential for security, see below. An indication of the effect (impact) of an incident is often used. If the impact directly jeopardises the fulfilment of the SLA, it will have a higher priority than incidents for which a workaround exists. When an incident is registered, a link is made as quickly as possible to the CI the incident concerns. The incident is given an incident number and this is provided to the incident reporter, in case he wishes to make any additional reports about the incident. If possible, the reporter is helped immediately, possibly with a temporary solution.

As mentioned, the output consists of immediate solutions or alternative ways of working. Incidents are registered in every case and these records form the input for the Problem Management process.

3.3.2.1   Incident Control/Help Desk and Security Management

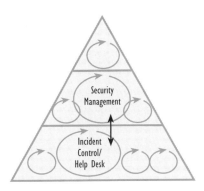

The Incident Control/Help Desk is the main liaison point for security incidents. In the procedural sense, security incidents are no different from any other incidents to the Incident Control/Help Desk, i.e., the incidents are registered and the proper procedure for dealing with them is selected (the categorisation of the incident). In the case of security incidents, depending on the incident's seriousness, a different procedure from that for normal incidents may apply. It is therefore essential for the Incident Control/Help Desk to recognise a security incident as such. Security incidents include all those incidents that may impede the fulfilment of the security requirements in the SLA. It is helpful if the SLA includes a summary of the types of incidents that have to be considered as security incidents. Security incidents are also those incidents that impede the achievement of the organisation's own basic level of security (baseline). As mentioned, the baseline is the level adopted by the IT organisation for its own security and from the point of view of good 'due diligence'.

Some typical examples of security incidents include:

- possible breaches of confidentiality requirements:
    - incidents that made unauthorised access to information possible
    - loss of data carriers off the premises
    - loss or theft of a laptop
    - attempts to acquire higher authorisation by the organisation's own staff
    - attempts from inside or outside to gain access to systems (hacking)

- possible breaches of integrity requirements:
    - loss of data or incomplete processing of transactions
    - viruses, Trojan horses (malicious software)
    - bad tracks on hard disks, parity errors in the memory
    - faulty checksums or hash values

- possible breaches of availability requirements:
    - interruption of the service for an unacceptable period. If the interruption lasts longer than a period agreed on in the SLA and cannot be rectified within a certain period, the contingency plan comes into effect. (This subject is dealt with under the Business Continuity Planning process)
    - viruses, Trojan horses (malicious software)
    - theft of laptops, components or data carriers.

Note that the reporting of security incidents will not always stem from users or IT personnel, but also from the management itself, on the basis of alarm reports or audit data from the systems, for example. Note also that for example the theft of a laptop is initially a breach of availability, but there are now potential breaches of confidentiality (disclosure of data held on the laptop) and integrity (data on laptop is modified or deleted or is virus infected). So the list of potential impacts of a single incident can become more complex.

As mentioned, it is essential for the Incident Control/Help Desk to recognise a security incident as such. Only then will it be possible to set in motion the correct procedure for dealing with security incidents. If the security incident concerns a CI with a higher classification, it may be necessary to follow a different procedure. For example, it may be necessary for the IT service provider's Security Manager to notify the customer's Security Officer. The customer's Security Officers serve as the points of contact between the customer and the provider in connection with security. Other follow-up activities may also be defined in the procedure, including reports to the customer. The problem is therefore concerned with how the Incident Control/Help Desk recognises a security incident. It is advisable to include examples of security incidents in the SLA. It is also advisable to lay down the procedure for various types of security incidents in the SLA.

A security incident may have to be treated as confidential in order to minimise the consequential losses, or to create better opportunities for discovering the cause of the security incident (but this must never be an excuse for not reporting a security incident!). It is therefore worthwhile considering classifying security incidents as well. It is always advisable to agree on a procedure about the communication concerning security incidents. It would not be for the first time that an organisation panics because of an exaggerated rumour. Nor would it be the first time that unnecessary losses were incurred because a security incident was reported too late. It is advisable for all the communication concerned with security incidents to take place via the *Security Manager*.

Describing the nature of a security incident is necessary but not in itself sufficient. There also has to be a certain level of security awareness among employees. This is dealt with in more detail in Chapter 5.

3.3.2.2 Security incident control

The handling of security incidents is important. Despite all efforts of devising and implementing measures, security incidents will happen. Whether it is the 'simple' disappearance of a mail shipment with crucial information, the third crash in a row of a batch job, a fire at the neighbours or a horror story on the Internet about the very platform you're using.

It might not always be clear whether an incident really is a security incident. However, there is one general rule for dealing with all uncertainty: when in doubt, treat it as a security incident.

Information security does not work if security incidents are not processed in an orderly manner. Part of the process of handling a security incident is to solve it by correcting whatever has to be corrected. Another part is initiating actions to prevent reoccurrence. Depending on the damage that stems from a security incident, this may involve introducing new security measures. It might also mean that sanctions are required to prevent repetition.

Every organisational unit should have a point where security incidents can be reported (Incident Control/Help Desk). At the same time, make people aware that they can also report to a point of contact one level up. The reason for this is that even security liaison points or managers have been known to cause security incidents.

Also consider accepting reports of security incidents anonymously. The report's submission has greater priority than persuading the reporter to give his name. Anonymity should, however, be an exception. Security incident reporting is part of the learning process: staff are to be applauded for reporting security incidents. The reporting process helps to determine where improvements in security are possible or required. Reporting incidents should not be something to be afraid of, but something employees do since it is normal and good for the business.

A procedure for security incident reporting which includes using a predefined form should be described in the security handbook. It will help ensure that important information is not forgotten and that the information is not submitted through the wrong channels.

Escalation is required at the moment that solving the security incident exceeds the authority of the organisational unit. For instance, pulling the plug on the network might have serious consequences for other parts of the organisation, or even for third parties. In order to escalate, it must be very clear that escalation is in order. The same simple decision tree as that used for problem solving is required, for example, whenever a security incident involves more than the individual organisational unit, or whenever a given period for solving the problem has passed. These rules have to be included in the security incident handling procedure and usage of this procedure must be ensured.

3.3.2.3   Security incident registration

In security incident handling, incident registration is important enough to be dealt with separately. The best stepping stone for implementing information security is a history of mishaps. Unfortunately, beginners in the security world never have an accurate idea about the things that did not work in the past. There may be logs, and an enthusiastic system manager may tell you that there is a history, but if you have ever seen logs then you will know that extracting trends from them is almost impossible.

Security incidents are registered as part of incident reporting (also see the Incident Control/Help Desk function). This involves recording and keeping at least the following data:

- date, time, report serial number
- date, time of security incident
- details of the reporter (optional; anonymous reports will be accepted)
- descriptive title
- detailed description
- estimate of damage (if appropriate)
- urgency
- organisational unit where the security incident occurred or was noticed
- system or infrastructure affected
- point of contact to ask questions/report result
- escalation status
- solution.

As mentioned before, having a history of security incidents enables an analysis of the effectiveness of measures, of the seriousness of the things that can go wrong, and of the trends, etc. It is a valuable Security Management instrument for Problem Management.

3.3.3   Problem Management

Problem Management attempts to discover the links between incidents, so that the cause of the incidents can be traced. This can be followed by measures to prevent the incidents from reoccurring. This approach also makes it possible to detect security "leaks". The Problem Management process is intended to manage, establish links and systematically solve the causes of and eliminate the incidents. If the cause of a problem is determined, a known error can be defined.

The output of the Problem Management process consists of known errors, and Requests for Changes (RFCs). An RFC is a proposal for a change in the IT infrastructure. The solutions are carefully documented and made accessible to the Incident Control/Help Desk under keywords. The known errors and the RFCs provide the input for the Change Management process.

3.3.3.1 Problem Management and Security Management

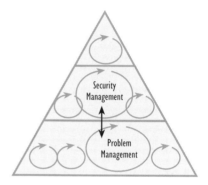

If a 'problem' arises from a security incident, it may be that a separate procedure has to be followed. A number of issues are particularly important:

- First and foremost consider the people who may be involved or who may know something about the security incident. This is because it is advisable to keep the group of people who know about the security incident as small as possible (loss of face, good reputation). Knowledge of a possible security leak should also be kept to the minimum to prevent the possibility of the knowledge being misused or the leak being exploited.

- Secondly, consider the people whom it is essential to involve in finding a solution for the security incident (the Security Manager of the IT service provider, and possibly the customer's Security Officer).

- The third test in preparing for a solution is to always ensure that no new security problems arise on account of the solution (test in terms of the fulfilment of the SLA and the organisation's own baseline).

3.3.4   Change Management Process

The goal of the Change Management process is to control and manage all the changes concerned with the CIs. Changes in the IT infrastructure always come about through this process. A change is a controlled change in the IT infrastructure.

The input for Change Management is formed by the known errors and Requests for Changes (RFCs).

The Change Manager has final responsibility for this process. Part of these activities involves drawing up, handling, processing and, after approval, (arranging for) building, testing and the implementation of a change. The output of this process is an evaluated and authorised change. Part of making the change itself involves updating the CI data in the CMDB by the Configuration and Asset Management process.

3.3.4.1   Change Management and Security Management

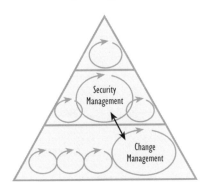

The activities in the Change Management process often show some relationship to security. After all, security and Change Management go hand-in-hand. If a situation is reached with an acceptable level of security, and this situation is controlled by the change process, it is possible for the organisation itself to ensure that the new situation has an acceptable level of security as well. Therefore, a number of fixed steps are distinguished to guarantee this level of security. Figure 3.6 shows the steps that have to be taken. The input is an RFC that includes a proposal to change the IT infrastructure, and provides the reasons and the references to the CIs concerned. Parameters are linked to an RFC that affect the acceptance procedure. The parameters in the figure are intended as an example; other choices are also possible. The choice here is a parameter for the urgency. The reasons for this could be that, without implementation, the SLA could no longer be fulfilled, neither now nor in the near future. An 'impact' parameter is also included, which expresses the impact on the IT configuration or its management. The 'impact on information security' parameter is also included. If the proposal could have a major impact on information security, more stringent acceptance tests and procedures would be necessary.

Security proposals also form part of the RFC. The starting point here is again the agreements contained in the SLA, as well as the security baseline chosen by the IT service provider. The general security profiles are often used, which specify which security measures have to be implemented for which types of products (see also Annex C). For example, the following have to be specified for each operating system: identification and authentication, authorisation, access control, audit/logging, and management (including user management and the management of rights). Security proposals therefore consist of a collection of security measures that are often combined in a procedure laid down in documentation.

The RFC is then assessed and authorised. In the case of RFCs with a limited impact, this can be carried out by the Change Manager or be delegated. In the case of an RFC with greater consequences, the decision is taken by the Change Advisory Board (CAB). The CAB always includes the Security Manager, and possibly also the Security Officer of the customer(s), if the RFC could have a major impact on security.

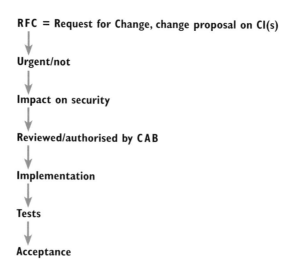

RFC = Request for Change, change proposal on CI(s)

↓

Urgent/not

↓

Impact on security

↓

Reviewed/authorised by CAB

↓

Implementation

↓

Tests

↓

Acceptance

Figure 3.6: A Change

It is not necessary to bring in the Security Manager for every change. As far as possible, security has to be an integrated part of normal tasks. This implies that security has to be in mind whenever changes to specifications occur. For instance what effects the change may have on security or whether security requirements are needed in addition to the change.

The Change Manager has to be in a position to assess whether an RFC will have a high impact on security, and whether he or the CAB needs input from the Security Manager. Nor is the Security Manager always required for the selection of measures for the CIs that are involved in the RFC. After all, if everything is in order, the framework for the measures being taken is ready and the only question is concerned with the way in which they have to be implemented.

As mentioned, in special cases the customer may be represented in the CAB by the Security Officer. The Security Officer is invited by the Change Manager, or the Security Manager.

In implementing the change it is therefore necessary to implement the security measures immediately and to then test them. Testing security is different from normal functional testing. Normal tests examine whether a particular function is present. When testing security the focus is not only on the presence and efficacy of a (security) function but also on the absence of other unwanted functions. The functions in the latter category generally account for the holes in the system.

The Change Advisory Board decides whether or not to accept an RFC. If the CAB approves, the RFC is authorised. The CAB's composition will depend on the expertise required to assess an RFC. This is the responsibility of the Change Manager. In the case of an RFC with a major impact on security, the CAB also includes the Security Manager of the IT service provider. Depending on the organisation and the nature of the RFCs, the CAB's composition may be as follows:

- Change Manager
- Architect
- Technical specialist
- Developer
- Operational Manager
- User representatives
- Security Manager.

From the security point of view, the Change Management process is one of the most important processes. After all, this is where new security measures are introduced into the IT infrastructure and existing measures are sharpened, along with the changes to the IT infrastructure. It is also where checks are made that other changes to systems are implemented without compromising the existing security environment.

Finally:

- The implementation of changes sometimes (too often) results in security incidents, with the associated problems that accompany them. Implementing changes on the basis of a plan (that is organising the changes), will reduce the negative consequences of changes in terms of disruptions.

- Change Management in general, and the CAB in particular, have to ensure that the level of security is not reduced by a change, and that it certainly does not fall below the agreed level. This is a point for special attention in the test procedures.

3.3.5   Release Management Process

The last process in the Service Support set to be discussed is the Release Management process. The goal of this process is to implement software version management and to arrange software distribution. The input for this process can be an authorised RFC out of the Change Management process. To this end, this process has what is called the Definitive Software Library. This is the repository of all the correct, recognised, registered, legal and authorised software, possibly with a reference to the source code, the depot or the installation files. This library need not be a separate database; it can just be a part of the CMDB.

3.3.5.1   Release Management and Security Management

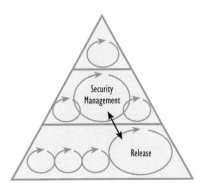

It is important that all software enters the organisation through this process in a controlled manner. This process ensures that:

- the correct software is used
- the software is tested in advance
- the introduction is authorised in the correct manner (by means of a change)
- the software is legal
- the software is imported virus free and remains virus free when distributed
- the version numbers are known (and registered by Configuration and Asset Management in the CMDB)
- the roll-out process is tested in advance

- it is possible to 'back out' and go back to the old situation
- controlled introduction is possible.

This process, too, operates according to a fixed set of procedures, with due attention being paid to information security. It is particularly important for the security implications to be considered during the testing and acceptance stage. This will ensure that the security requirements and measures identified in the SLA will not be compromised.

3.4 The Service Delivery set and Security Management

This section describes the relationships of the processes in the Service Delivery set with the Security Management process. The Availability Management process and the Business Continuity Planning process are especially important for the Security Management process. For the reader's convenience, Annex A includes a list of cross-references between the Code of Practice for Information Security Management and these processes, as well as what can reasonably be expected from these processes in terms of security.

3.4.1 Service Level Management

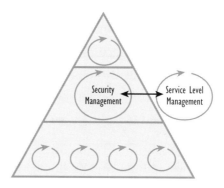

Service Level Management ensures that agreements on the services supplied to customers are specified and fulfilled. The goal is to create an IT service of the optimum level: i.e. the wishes and requirements of the customers of the IT services are fulfilled and that the associated costs can be justified for both the provider and the customer.

The Service Level Agreements must also include agreements about the security measures to be taken. (See framework for a security section in Annex B.)

Service Level Management makes a distinction between a number of connected activities that have to be examined from the security point of view:

- identification of the security requirements and wishes of the customer
- verification of the feasibility of these security requirements and the wishes of the customer
- negotiation of proposals and recording of the required level of security of the IT services
- determining, drawing up and establishing security standards for the IT service
- monitoring those security standards
- reporting on the effectiveness and status of security of IT services provided.

The starting point when establishing the SLA is often that a general level of security exists (the basic level of security, or baseline). It must be explicitly laid down in the SLA if a customer wants a higher level of security.

3.4.2   Availability Management

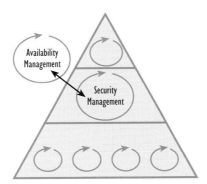

Availability Management is concerned with the technical availability of IT components. It manages the information security in terms of the availability criterion. The quality aspect of availability is guaranteed by other quality aspects, namely, reliability, maintainability, serviceability and resilience. The reliability of an IT service indicates the degree to which the service offers the agreed functionality during an indicated period. Maintainability is an indication of the ease with which maintenance can be carried out on a service, on the basis of prescribed methods and techniques. Serviceability of an IT service means the way contracts with third parties about the availability of their IT components are dealt with. Resilience is the ability of an IT service to continue to operate properly, in spite of the malfunctioning of one or more subsystems.

Clearly, Availability Management is closely connected with Security Management: departures from the IT service level, for example when an IT service is not available, may be caused by a security incident.

3.4.3   Performance and Capacity Management

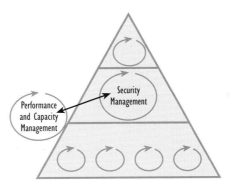

Performance and Capacity Management is responsible for the optimum deployment of IT resources, as agreed with the customer. The performance requirements are derived from the qualitative and quantitative standards that are drawn up in the Service Level Management process.

Practically all the activities in the Performance and Capacity Management process are related to Security Management:

- Performance management: monitoring and improving performance in terms of throughput capacity and response times. This activity can provide a mine of information, which, when analysed, may reveal security incidents.

- Resource management: providing an insight into the IT infrastructure and its use. Managing data storage space may, for example, provide information about the storage of undesirable data. Assessing new technologies from the point of view of security may reveal some interesting information.

- Demand management: a control activity to influence the use of IT services. If the demand for capacity is spread out, a decision may be taken to establish certain extra security requirements, or alternatively to reduce them to a baseline level.

- Workload management: determines and monitors what a system gets to process as a result of the processing of applications. Significant departures from the normal daily workload may, but do not necessarily, indicate security incidents.

- Application sizing: estimates the resources required for an application. If these specifications are not available, it will sometimes be necessary to turn to suppliers. The specifications they provide should always be checked for accuracy and the security risks involved.

- Modelling: models make it possible to set up a number of security scenarios and to make various 'what if' analyses.

3.4.4   Business Continuity Planning

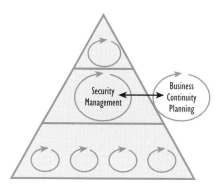

Business Continuity Planning ensures that, if a disaster occurs, its consequences for IT services are limited to a level agreed with the customer. With the ever increasing dependency on IT, it is important that IT services are consistently delivered to an agreed level of quality. Every time a service is degraded or unavailable, customers are unable to continue with their normal business. It is therefore important that the effects of losing the use of IT systems is assessed.

This is why it is imperative that contingency plans are made in order to ensure the continued operation of the business and also to provide the ability to successfully recover computer services in the event of a disaster. The contingency plan also gives clear guidance how and when this plan should be invoked.

3.4.5 Financial Management and Costing

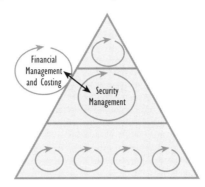

The aim of Financial Management and Costing is to understand and monitor costs and charge the costs to the customers of the IT services. To manage effectively and to plan ahead accurately, it is essential that a business has detailed knowledge of the costs incurred, and identification of where resources have been used. Financial Management and Costing is the process that delivers relevant organisational and financial data, so that on any organisational level an optimal balance can be made between price and achievements. It gives an insight into how well any IT Service Management process is carried out against reasonable costs. The effective implementation of Financial Management and Costing in an organisation can avoid over ambition and correct levels of affordable achievements.

In practice Financial Management and Costing deals with two main activities: costing and charging. Costing is the identification, allocation, prediction and monitoring of costs involved in the delivery of IT services. Costing is internally focused on the IT department itself. Charging is the way the costs of the IT services are accounted to the users. So charging is more externally focused on the users of IT services.

Financial Management and Costing gives an insight into the costs involved for some of the security measures. Most of the costs however are hidden or inherently related to management of the general IT infrastructure. For some security measures, such as the introduction of a firewall, the management of user rights, or the use of an anti-virus product, Financial Management and Costing can give the required insight.

3.5 ITIL and security, together a controlled process

Security and management are concepts that are symbiotic. Security depends on management and management is impossible without proper security.

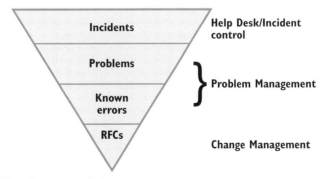

Figure 3.7: ITIL and Security – a controlled process

Figure 3.7 shows a triangle with, at the top, a relatively large number of incidents, where the security incidents have to be recognised by the Incident Control/Help Desk function. An appropriate response is required for serious incidents. In addition, there is an insight into the effectiveness of the security measures on the basis of a total overview of all the security incidents. Problem Management takes over the issues that cannot be solved immediately and either solves the problem, taking into account the preconditions for security set by the SLA and the basic level of security, or it identifies a known error. This is followed by the Change Management process, in which controlled modifications of the IT infrastructure are made on the basis of Requests for Changes (RFCs). Part of this control also involves taking the necessary security measures and maintaining the agreed level of security.

Because the use of ITIL gives rise to a controlled process, there will also be fewer errors in management and security. This is a major benefit for security. Many incidents are in fact caused by misunderstandings or errors. The next chapter explains how Security Management can also be implemented on the basis of a process, and in accordance with the ITIL concept.

4 SECURITY MANAGEMENT MEASURES

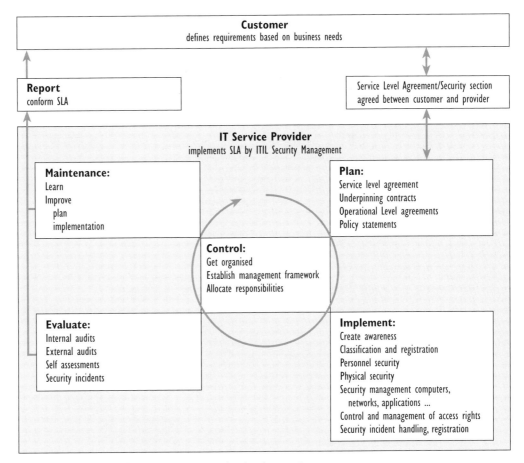

Figure 4.1: The Security Management process showing the security measures

Figure 4.1 above replicates that shown in Chapter 2, which describes the Security Management process as a whole. Chapter 3 described how the Security Management process is based on and connected with the other ITIL processes. This chapter provides a general overview of the security measures themselves, which are implemented through the Security Management process. As an aid to drawing up an SLA, Annex A shows the same measures in tabular form.

These measures are based on the most recent version (1999) of the Code of Practice for Information Security Management (Guidelines for Management and Implementation), BS7799, developed by the British Standards Institute. The Code of Practice contains a common set of Generally Accepted Security Practices (GASP). The Code essentially instils a framework on how IT security is to be approached. The Code of Practice is widely accepted as a common reference source for security baselines. The Code of Practice covers all items known from the Internet Site Security Handbook, but in a more general manner, and those of the USA National Institute for Standards and Technology (NIST) guidelines on information security.

The text contains various key controls, or key measures. These are the most important measures according to the Code of Practice for Information Security Management.

This chapter follows Figure 4.1, with the exception of the PLAN-block which is dealt with in Chapter 2 and in Annex C:

- the 'CONTROL' block in the centre of the figure shows the organisation of information security
- the 'IMPLEMENT' block covers:
  - assets classification and control
  - security requirements vis-à-vis personnel
  - physical security
  - secure computer and network management
  - system access control and user access management
- the 'EVALUATE' block covers the EDP audit, or the IT systems security checks
- the 'MAINTENANCE' block describes how to learn from the past experiences and improve both the plan or the implementation thereof
- finally, the 'REPORT' block describes the reporting structure.

4.1   Control

4.1.1   Organisation of information security

4.1.1.1   Objective

To manage information security in order to facilitate secure operation by the IT service provider. Establish a management framework to initiate and manage information security in the organisation. Establish an organisation structure to prepare, approve and implement the information security policy, to allocate responsibilities and to actually implement the security measures. If necessary, create particular jobs for information security specialists.

4.1.1.2   Summary of measures

- Establishment of a 'Management forum for information security': this forum can be composed of the jointly responsible line managers, plus employees with specialist security roles (who can also make the preparations for forum meetings). The forum meets several times a year, for example as part of an extended normal management team meeting, to give direction to information security. The typical tasks of such a forum would be: to review the policy, modify security measures (the framework of standards), approve security plans, maintain responsibilities, and to monitor changing threats and incidents.

- Information security co-ordination: this refers to implementing plans and measures; agreements about co-operation and the co-ordination between the various roles and responsibilities relating to information security; agreements about the methods and techniques to be used (for example, the method used for risk analysis and the use of a single classification system throughout the organisation); setting up organisation-wide initiatives (for example a security awareness program).

- Allocation of information security responsibilities: clearly define the responsibilities, including those for the protection of data, information systems and for implementing particular security procedures.

- Authorisation process for IT facilities: before IT facilities enter the operational phase, carry out tests or audits and ensure that the security is in order. The operational phase is only entered after authorisation by the manager concerned.

- Specialist advice: where necessary, obtain advice in specialist areas, for example in connection with risks, audits or technical security measures.

- Co-operation between organisations: in the security world, it is a good practice to ensure there is co-operation and co-ordination between organisations as well as security specialists about security matters that concern everyone, for example new methodologies, but also changing threats.

- Independent review: ensure that the implementation of information security is regularly reviewed by an independent party, for example, the internal or external (EDP or IT) auditor.

- Security of third party access: identify the risks arising from links with third parties (using risk analysis). Supplementary measures may be taken, see Annex B.

- Contracts: contracts with third parties (including the Service Level Agreements and Interchange Agreements) should include security conditions, see also Annex B.

4.2 Implement

4.2.1 Asset classification and control

4.2.1.1 Objective

To provide an approach for implementing security measures and maintaining the protection of organisational assets.

4.2.1.2 Summary of measures

- Accountability for assets: ensure there is an overview of the most important information sources and systems (the information assets); allocate responsibility for all information and systems. Other assets include software (applications), hardware, documentation and procedures. The asset list or asset management system can be integrated with the CMDB.

- Information classification: rules for classification are drawn up outside the sphere of ITIL: in the user organisation. The information classification itself is also done outside the IT service provider organisation. If this involves the implementation of particular classification rules, implementation can be made a task of the IT service provider, by means of the SLA. A classification system helps in determining the need for, and level of, security measures. It is good practice to make a distinction in the classification system between confidentiality, integrity and availability.

- Guidelines: attention to guidelines for the classification itself (insofar as the IT service provider is responsible for the implementation: details of how to implement, who is responsible for implementation, whether or not physical labels are used, how long a classification remains valid, and so forth).

4.2.2 Personnel security

4.2.2.1 Objective

To make the best possible use and to maintain the required level of knowledge and experience of the employees, in order to promote security, as well as to reduce the risks that may arise from intentional and unintentional human actions.

4.2.2.2 Summary of measures

- Job descriptions: include security roles and responsibilities in job descriptions.
- Screening: screen applicants for jobs involving sensitive information.
- Confidentiality agreement: ensure that employees (including temporary) sign a confidentiality (non-disclosure) agreement, as part of their initial conditions of employment.
- Training for all personnel: make employees aware of the security threats and of the importance of information security, and equip them with the proper resources, knowledge and skills. Train employees in security procedures and techniques. Insofar as it is relevant, this also applies to third parties, for example employment agency workers.
- Responding to security incidents: report security incidents as quickly as possible through the right channels. The appropriate response to security incidents can limit the damage. Security incident reports also provide greater insight into the effectiveness of the system of security measures. Incidents are reported to the Incident Control/Help Desk and it must be capable of recognising security incidents (i.e. incidents that may impede the fulfilment of the SLA) and must have procedures for responding to security incidents.
- Security weaknesses: encourage employees to report security weaknesses (also in software) and 'near misses'.

- Disciplinary measures: besides the activities concerned with encouraging employee security awareness, implement a procedure for taking disciplinary measures against employees who deliberately or persistently behave in a way that is detrimental to the organisation's security or against the organisation's security policy.

- Security awareness: this is the most important and most difficult challenge in information security. See 5.1.

4.2.3 Communications and operations management

The precise shape given to the management of computers depends very much on the organisation, the importance of the information systems for the various business processes, and, of course, the nature and sensitivity of the business applications. The measures needed by a large organisation with a large number of mainframe applications will be different from those needed by a small organisation. However, the same basic principles will apply, which are all concerned with making risks manageable.

4.2.3.1 Objective

To ensure the proper, correct use and secure operation of IT resources.

4.2.3.2 Summary of measures

- Operational procedures and responsibilities: ensure there are established responsibilities for the management of *all* IT resources and *all* parts of the IT infrastructure (and a procedure for maintaining responsibilities).

- Documented operating procedures: draw up procedures for the management of operations. In particular, take into account segregation of duties and security incident handling.

- Incident management procedures: draw up procedures and establish responsibilities for handling security incidents. This includes security incident reporting which has already been dealt with above.

- Segregation of duties: segregate duties and tasks so that they are carried out by several people. This reduces the possibility of security incidents occurring through human error (achieved for example by separating implementation and supervisory duties) and reduces the possibility of misuse or fraud (effective segregation of duties means that more employees have to conspire with each other to be able to commit fraud). Segregation of duties is not a goal in itself but should be implemented based on an identified need, for specific functions and for specific situations.

- Separation of development and production: keep the development phase and the production phase of an information system organisationally and technically separate. This is to minimise the likelihood of disruptions in the production environment and to impede the undesirable use of authorisations for system development in the production environment, thus also reducing the possibilities for fraud.

- External facilities management: there are no fundamental differences between the situation in which facilities management is in the hands of the organisation's own people and when it is in the hands of an external contractor. A certain level of service and security is expected in either case. However, a possible shift in threats has to be taken into account (as other people may gain access to your information), and possible conflicts of interest may arise in a customer and supplier relationship. Likewise, or especially, in a situation where the facilities management is placed in the hands of an external contractor, draw up the security measures in a form that can also serve as a testing framework (standards) for the required level of performance. The Code can therefore be used to specify, co-ordinate and verify the security measures and standards.

■ Handling and security of data carriers: avoid damage to organisational assets and interruptions to the production process by protecting the physical data carriers, such as computer tapes, floppy disks and hard disks and also documents, memo tapes, videos or any other types of data carriers. Pay particular attention to:

- the management and security of removable computer media
- the procedures for using and handling data carriers (including guidelines for keeping duplicates and making backups, keeping more generations of data, and procedures for on-site and off-site storage of data carriers, including backups)
- the security of system documentation or other documentation that may provide information about vulnerable areas
- the re-use and disposal of old data carriers
- the establishment of an agreement when data is regularly exchanged with third parties (interchange agreement)

■ Network management: security measures for networks require the same approach as that described above for computer management. The problem may be special in terms of the different nature of the threats (especially with regard to confidentiality and continuity), the shared use of the infrastructure (friend and foe share the same medium), the use of external services and the involvement of other people with commanding roles. Using additional measures, such as encryption techniques, may be considered on the basis of a risk analysis.

■ Network services: it is necessary to take appropriate security measures if network services are used for exchanging information, such as EDI or e-mail. The measures can be laid down in an Interchange Agreement (or, for internal use, guidelines). For internal use, 'groupware' applications are becoming more common, which include the electronic office and the electronic agenda. Assess these developments (and in fact *all* changes in the use of IT) in terms of their impact on the nature of the threats, the dependencies, and how they are embedded in the current organisation.

4.2.4 Access control

4.2.4.1 Objective

To prevent unauthorised access to information and information systems in order to protect the confidentiality of the information, to prevent unauthorised and undesirable changes, damage or destruction of information or software, and to prevent disruptions in the normal production process. A distinction is made between access security in relation to networks, computers and applications.

4.2.4.2 Summary of measures

■ Maintenance of effective control over access: ensure that effective control over access is maintained and includes the management of users, accounts, rights, means of identification and authentication (including passwords and tokens) and keeping access rights up-to-date.

■ End-user responsibilities are, of course, the responsibility of the customer's organisation. Encourage customer organisations to address their responsibilities more explicitly in the SLA. There is a framework in Annex B for the security section in the SLA, and this can be used for this purpose. Column 'H' in Table B.1 is intended for setting out the customer's and end-user's responsibilities for security. Whether or not security is effective depends on the co-operation of the users. Encouraging security awareness is essential here. Pay specific attention to the user responsibilities for the use of passwords, for not leaving active sessions, equipment and data carriers unattended, procedures for import and export of software and data carriers (to prevent viruses and illegal software), use of external sources (Internet and other external data communication), backups (e.g. of laptops) and other user responsibilities for laptop usage. User responsibilities are given in more detail in Annex A.

■ Network access control. The choice of security measures in a network depends very much on the situation. The most important measures for access security in network situations are indicated below:

– Control access rights and restrictions to network services for internal as well as external users, i.e. for both 'incoming' and 'outgoing' services: as a rule, always authenticate users (particularly in dial-up situations).

– Networks can be separated and facilities are possible for access control between these 'network domains' (for example by controlling the connection possibilities by using dial-up facilities, bridges or routers); it's also possible to create an enforced path through the domains.

– As far as is technically possible, identify and authenticate computer systems, workstations and PCs in the network.

– Control securely remote management, particularly in relation to diagnostic ports.

– Third party network services: determine the security requirements on the basis of a risk analysis and set out these requirements in an agreement, such as a Service Level Agreement. Choose a form for this that is readily controllable.

■ Computer access control also depends very much on the possibilities for identification and authentication. The most important measures for computer access control are indicated below:

– Identify and authenticate all workstations and terminals.

– Enforce a standard Logon procedure in which the minimum of information is provided (e.g. avoid providing details of the system type or organisation name).

– Always identify and authenticate the end user. The activities in the information system concerned with this should be traceable to a natural person, in order to assist auditing. Identification can be based on, for example, passwords, smart cards or tokens.

– Duress alarm: consider the installation of a duress alarm on the basis of a risk analysis. This enables authorised users to indicate if they are being forced to carry out an action. An example is being forced to implement a transaction whereby, instead of using the normal Login procedure, another procedure under the user's name for 'duress alarm' is used.

– Automatic time-out: after a fixed period of inactivity, an automatic time-out facility cuts off a workstation or user, or the user is logged off.

- Time slots: limit the use of IT resources to normal office hours, for example 8:00 hours to 19:00 hours.
- Lock-out after a fixed number of failed access attempts.
- Implement more stringent log-in checks for off-site access including dial back, and authentication based on a token or smart card and/or a challenge and response mechanism.

■ Application access control: achieve a more precise form of security by using 'roles' and 'functions' in the applications themselves. For example, the function 'prepare a transaction' can be executed by a different employee from the one who executes the 'authorise the transaction' function. This segregation of duties reduces the likelihood of fraud, and increases the likelihood of detection. Besides this type of access control of application system functions, access security can also be applied to system help, libraries and the files of the programs themselves (the *executables*). In the case of very sensitive information systems, a dedicated (isolated) computing environment, i.e. without any shared facilities, might provide the simplest and safest solution.

■ Anti-virus control policy. Where anti-virus software is chosen, this needs to include regular updating at both the server and the client and take care to ensure that it is appropriate to the operating system(s) in use. Note that this must include stand-alone desktop and laptop equipment, where consideration also has to be given to how the drivers will be updated. You need to:

- determine how frequently the various levels of software need to be updated
- ensure that you purchase the correct number and type of licences not forgetting the special needs of the Internet/e-mail
- monitor the receipt of the updates
- manage the updating process for both the networked and stand-alone systems remembering that you may need to take special steps to monitor whether remote equipment is being properly updated – see the ITIL book Release Management.

■ Monitoring and auditing information system access and use: take the following measures to detect unauthorised activities (see also the next section on auditing):

- audit trail, warning: record exceptional or suspicious events (possible security incidents) in an audit trail; which may be combined with a direct warning to the system manager or Security Officer
- monitoring system use: monitor system use and consider the possibility of generating a warning when established limits are exceeded
- clock synchronisation: it is advisable to synchronise system clocks from the point of view of interpreting audit data and collecting evidence
- virus attacks: set up a procedure for staff to pass on reports from the anti-virus software that it has blocked attempts at virus infection, including, if possible, an indication of the source for remedial action.

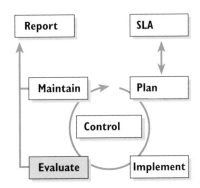

| 4.3 | Audit and Evaluate: Security reviews of IT systems |

4.3.1 Objective

To supervise (check) compliance with the security policy of the organisation of the customer(s) and compliance with the agreed standards (usually in the SLA). This requires a regular audit of the technical security of the IT systems. The IT service provider supplies information for this to an independent EDP auditor (also called IT auditor) or the customer's EDP auditor.

4.3.2 Summary of measures

- Undesirable use of IT facilities: focus on preventing undesirable use or even misuse of the resources placed at the disposal of employees. Only permit use for authorised business objectives, covered by the job description of the employee. The same limitation applies to the use of resources *by* and *of* third parties. This includes, for example, not only those activities that may be covered by legislation on computer crime, but also the improper use of IT facilities, such as playing computer games or keeping private accounts. Include in the SLA details of what is expected of the IT service provider in this area.

- Compliance with security policy and standards: regularly check compliance with the security policy, the security standards and any other security requirements taking into account the effectiveness and efficiency of the policy and the system of security measures.

- Legal compliance, including prevention of illegal copying of software.

- Security reviews of IT systems: regularly check the compliance with the technical security standards for IT facilities.

- EDP audits: carefully plan and execute the audits in the IT environment so that the organisation and responsibilities are clear; the audit activities are laid down and interference with production is kept to the minimum. The knowledge and level of experience of the EDP auditors must be monitored.

- Only make audit tools available to authorised employees.

4.4   Maintenance

4.4.1   Objective

To provide input to:

- improve on agreements on security as specified in, e.g., the security parts in the SLA, the OLAs, and the underpinning contracts
- improve implementation of specified security measures.

4.4.2   Summary of measures

- analysis of the evaluation reports
- providing input for the security plan(s) and the yearly improvement activities
- providing input for the SLA maintenance activities (for the Service Level Manager) as well as for the maintenance activities on OLAs and underpinning contracts.

4.5   Report

4.5.1   Objective

To provide the customers with relevant information on information security.

4.5.2   Summary of measures

In general, the Security Management process provides reporting data to the Service Level Management process. Service Level Management takes care of the communication with the customer.

Possible regular reports and reportable events:

- Reports on the Plan activity:
  - reports on conformance to the SLA including the agreed upon KPIs for security
  - reports on underpinning contracts and any disconformities in their fulfilment
  - reports on Operational Level Agreements and policy statements

- Regular reports on the Implementation activity:
  - status of information security like implemented measures, education and reviews including self assessments and risk analyses
  - overview of security incidents and the reaction to these incidents – this compared to a previous time frame
  - status of awareness programs
  - trends on incidents per system, per process, per department, etc.

- Reports on, and of, the Evaluate activity:
  - results of audits, reviews and internal assessments
  - warnings, new threats, et cetera

- Specific Reportable events:
  - for certain security incidents, the Incident Control/Help Desk and the Security Manager do have a direct channel to the customer's representative. This goes beyond the normal reporting procedures.

5 GUIDELINES FOR IMPLEMENTING SECURITY MANAGEMENT

Some real life examples:

An automobile concern discovered it had lost important computer files, after a Security Officer set out to prove that computer system security was inadequate, and brought the head office to a standstill. The Security Officer succeeded in this demonstration but the management of the organisation was faced with the need to take recovery measures and a great deal of negative publicity.

An American company discovered that 160,000 records had suddenly gone missing. The reason was a small, destructive program, a logical bomb, left in the organisation's computers by an ex-employee who wanted to get even.

In a large city, the subway stopped working one day. A virus was discovered in the computer systems which controlled the points of the railway.

A major European stock exchange was stopped because of a computer error. This was caused by a procedural error, effecting the capacity limit during the day. In order to overcome this, trading had to be stopped for two hours.

Because of the failure of an electricity company's computer, a big part of a county in the Netherlands did not have streetlights for one and a half hours.

An unknown end user drinking hot chocolate spilt some and made a mess of the keyboard. As a result the standalone computer used for surfing the Internet was unavailable for a customer that wanted to look for a new job.

5.1 Awareness

Information security is considered the biggest challenge management will face during the next decade. Measures are seldom readily accepted and resistance to them is the rule rather than the exception. Measures cost money and the return on investment is difficult to assess. Users don't like having their privileges removed, even when they are not really required. Having privileges gives them status, they think.

This means it is necessary to motivate users and management to exercise discipline in adhering to measures. Appeal for professionalism is the key. Remember that IT systems are often insecure, not for lack of good techniques but for lack of correct application of these techniques. Therefore, it all comes down to the attitudes and behaviour of people. Consequently, whenever possible, integrate security procedures into the normal everyday routine, and staff should come to recognise security as an enabler rather than a barrier.

Awareness campaigns will typically be an output from the Security Officer. However, maintenance will still rest with the Security Manager. Awareness and communication are the key terms. Explain to employees why security is needed and why certain security measures are taken. This will prevent the situation occurring where security creates barriers.

What kinds of awareness measures can be taken:

- Full-blown PR campaigns are used to improve awareness. It pays to implement an awareness program designed by a professional PR agency, such as the organisation's own PR department. The most effective way seems to be an annual communication plan, in which one subject is chosen for a period of approximately 2-3 months in order to inform the organisation about the background and the results.

- Make sure that employees appreciate the benefits of security to their organisation, themselves and their working environment. This includes taking steps to ensure that the measures fit well within the working environment, are not unnecessarily intrusive and are within the user's capabilities. Furthermore, users should be able to participate in the Security Management process where possible, e.g. to contribute to self-assessments, to improve on security measures and to report security incidents.

- Besides the use of good reports, using the corporate magazine to inform employees about mishaps, and the response to them, has proved to be effective.

- One of the more effective tricks is to display a readout at the entrance to the company restaurant showing the results of the different departments.

- Make clear to everyone that there is a single liaison point to address all possible emerging security problems: the Security Officer. Also make clear which meetings deal with the effectiveness and control of security measures.

- Ensure the security procedures are integrated into normal everyday mechanisms. Discipline and an awareness of why the procedures exist are essential. The former cannot be required without the latter. Few organisations have any means of enforcing discipline. Policing in whatever form can help, but experience shows that this can be costly and is not always effective. Demonstrating weaknesses or imposing sanctions on people may temporarily alert those who are involved, but the resulting awareness is usually short-lived. Security awareness is more readily influenced by clearly visible supervision (i.e. the security man on the front desk who asks you to open your briefcase on leaving the office, the key card you need to get into a closed computer centre) and by applying positive stimuli (i.e. include security awareness in job profiles).

- Draw up a communication plan in which you elaborate on how you will get your security policy across. In the communication plan you should address:
  - your mission and 'core message'
  - target groups
  - set up a communication structure: define who should communicate with whom and about which subjects
  - time scales
  - methods of communication: i.e. regular newsletters, awareness programs, leaflets, messages when employees log on to their system
  - target group identity goals, objectives, benefits, success and failure factors, and possible resistance.

5.2 Organisation of Security Management

Security Management remains a source of controversy. Although most people seem to agree on the objectives of Security Management, there is less consensus about the way to achieve the objectives. Security Management is divided into two schools: proponents of tailor-made security on the one side and proponents of ready-made security on the other. The former school argues that any type of security should start with a thorough investigation of dependencies, threats and weaknesses (risk analysis) and the latter school argues that efficiency dictates the use of checklists.

In implementing Security Management, it is important to take into account that:

- Information security implies making choices.
- Information security is cyclic.
- Security cycles occur at all levels in the organisation.

5.2.1 Making choices

An organisation's management has to make choices about which risks to cover, which measures to take, both now and in the next budgeting round. A proper risk analysis is a precondition for making these choices.

5.2.2 A cyclical system

Organisations and their information systems change. Checklists are often static and therefore fail to pay adequate attention to the rapid changes taking place in IT. Therefore, Security Management has to be continually revised, if it is to remain effective. Like any other management process, Security Management is a cyclical system: a never ending cycle of planning and checking as already shown in Chapter 2.

5.2.3 Security at all levels

The allocation of tasks in an organisation goes hand-in-hand with a transfer of powers and responsibilities from the senior management to the lower levels. Three levels are recognised in the literature:

- *Strategic*: this is where the organisation's objectives are determined, along with an outline of the method to use in achieving them. This is known as the general organisation policy. This is therefore the level at which to formulate the security policy.

- *Tactical*: this is where the organisation's basic policy is translated into an appropriate organisation structure and into specific plans that describe which processes have to be executed, which assets have to be deployed and what the outcome of the processes should be. This is the level where decisions are taken about the functional separation of development and management in a computer centre or the implementation of procedures for Change Management.

- *Operational*: this is the level at which the plans are actually executed, so that the organisation's objectives determined at the strategic level can be achieved within a specified time. This is the level at which password changes are made, authorisation is regulated and a firewall is configured.

5.2.4 Management – the role of the Security Manager

The Security Manager is the person who is responsible for the Security Management process. The Security Officers are the Security Manager's point of contact in the user organisation (the customers). The Security Manager's role must be clearly specified. There are various systems for determining roles and functions. The method used here conforms with the generally accepted standards of the NGI (Dutch acronym for the Netherlands association for IT professionals).

This methodology distinguishes between the following characteristics: type, knowledge, skills and experience. In addition to this, there is the mandate for the management role.

5.2.4.1 Type of person

The Security Manager is someone with a strong sense of responsibility, along with a healthy degree of scepticism. In view of the sensitivity of the task, the person should be extremely trustworthy, have an understanding of the politics of relationships and be able to weigh the feasible against the necessary.

5.2.4.2 Knowledge

The Security Manager must also have extensive knowledge of ICT, as well as typical security knowledge and a knowledge of financial reporting. A knowledge of the most relevant processes is also a requirement.

5.2.4.3 Skills

Besides management qualities, a sense of PR and tactical skills are required.

5.2.4.4 Experience

The role of Security Manager is an important one in the organisation. The person must have experience at the senior management level, be familiar with information security issues and have had at least ten years' experience in the IT business.

5.2.4.5 Mandate

The Security Manager does not need a special mandate from management and therefore need not be part of management. However, the manager does need the authority to issue instructions to the workforce during security incidents and, if necessary, to take immediate action, without having to ask for senior management's permission.

5.2.4.6 Screening

The Security Manager is acquainted with all the security plans and their strengths and weaknesses and also has an extensive knowledge of the business processes. This makes screening at a more senior level essential.

5.2.5 The Security Manager versus the Security Officer

The Security Manager is responsible for the Security Management process. This is a role and not necessarily a function, which is part of the supplier function, as opposed to the Security Officer, which is part of the customer function. The Security Manager is responsible for fulfilling the security demands as specified in the SLA, either directly or through delegation by the Service Level Manager. The generic security demands are fulfilled in specific security measures per systems and/or per unit in the IT service provider's organisation. These measures are documented in the security implementation plans. The Security Manager generally uses one of the many methods for risk analysis but proper results will only appear when the person is properly trained and has sufficient experience. Specifying the security measures in detail also requires an active role in the Change Management process and in the Change Advisory Board (CAB). Furthermore, the Security Manager is involved in handling specific security incidents and problems related to security, but in general is not involved personally in the implementation of security measures, nor in drawing up the handbooks.

Reporting is one of the tasks of the Security Manager (see section 4.5). These reports include results of self-assessments, internal EDP audits (IT audits) and progress reports. In addition, independent checking of the security plans and their proper implementation is done by independent EDP auditors.

The counterpart of the Security Manager in the customer's organisation is the Security Officer. The tasks of a Security Officer include:

- acting as the intermediary between the Security Manager and the business
- co-ordinating escalation in the case of (specific) security incidents
- co-ordinating the security measures to be implemented on the user's side (including authorization procedures, guidelines on the use of passwords, screen locking, clear desk, etc.)
- acting as interpreter of the official corporate security policy and intermediary between this and the business units, and advises with respect to the security requirements to be specified in the SLA.

The Security Officer co-ordinates assessing the business risks (the assessment itself is performed by the managers of the business units). The Security Manager may contact the Security Officer directly or through the Service Level Manager.

5.3 Documentation

A documentation framework is required to aid in standardisation and prevent inconsistencies. It provides sufficient leeway to avoid curtailing management – having excessive rules and regulations denies management the freedom to manage.

The documentation framework consists of three layers of documentation: the information security policy document, information security plans and handbooks for information security.

The security policy is defined for the organisation as a whole. The policy document provides guidance for all employees responsible for information security. Senior management should issue this document, which should contain, as a minimum:

- objectives and scope of information security for the organisation
- goals and management principles, including the way information security is being managed
- a definition of roles and responsibilities for information security
- the relationship with specific (security) policies and guidelines.

See Annex B for more details about the contents of a policy document

The security plan describes how the policy is implemented for a specific system and/or organisational unit. Annex C describes in more detail how a security plan can be drawn up. The security plan describes the desired situation, that is, the set of security measures that should be taken.

Finally, the handbooks describe the measures for guiding employees, either per system or per functional role. The handbooks describe the specific working instructions in detail and operational documents for day-to-day usage.

A framework can be developed using the above concept to provide a structure for the documents that describe information security. Using a structure provides overall consistency.

The overview in Table 5.1 shows the place of various documents within this documentation framework.

Table 5.1: Position of documents within documentation framework

	Corporate	**Department**	**Team**
Why	Policy		
What	Standards, plan	Standards, plan	
How		Handbook, procedures	Working instructions

Furthermore, to support the management cycle for information security, the following document structure also exists:

- The policy document, see Table 5.1

- Documentation that describes the current situation, derived from self-assessment, internal or external audits. The current situation is described both:
  - for the organisation as a whole (where it describes the progress of implementation of the security policy) and
  - per unit within the organisation or system (where it describes the implementation of the security plan)

- The periodic (e.g. yearly) information security improvement plans. These plans describe improvement activities and corrective actions either for the organisation as a whole (to improve implementation of the policy) or for specific organisational units or information systems (to improve implementation of the security plan).

Note that in the literature, the improvement plans are sometimes referred to as security plans. In this book, the security plans describe the desired situation (the set of measures that should be implemented), where security improvement plans describe how to get from the current to the desired situation.

5.4 Security Management for small and medium enterprises

For every organisation, small or big, it is crucial to have a security policy. This policy must be endorsed by top management, within the business organisation, in order to form part of the work ethic of the organisation. The organisation's security policy statement therefore becomes the foundation, and authority, for all lower level security policies. This policy and its derivatives like security measures may vary in complexity and scope. Most organisations will not have implemented all the security measures mentioned in section 4. There is no ready-made solution for Security Management. Which security measures are implemented is dependent on an organisation's own defined quality requirements, the baseline of Security Management it wants and the threats to the IT services in the organisation itself. Every organisation, small or big, has its own business targets. An important question is: "to what level is the general management willing to free-up resources for Security Management?"

There are common key areas for security measures which every organisation needs to deal with. These key areas are personnel, organisation, information, financial accounting, building and general affairs (electricity, water, fire etc.).

In general, implement the following controls as a start, no matter how small an organisation is:

- information security policy document
- allocation of information security responsibilities
- information security education and training
- reporting of security incidents
- virus controls
- business continuity planning process
- control of proprietary software copying
- safeguarding of organisational records
- data protection
- compliance with the security policy.

5.5 Pitfalls and success factors

As a humorous aside the list of stages of how Security Management should *not* be managed is (i) start with wild enthusiasm, which leads to (ii) confusion, resulting in (iii) disillusionment, followed by (iv) a search for the guilty party (v) punishment of the innocent and (vi) promotion of the non participants....

The most common negative attitudes of management to the implementation of Security Management are that:

- It costs money and it delivers no direct benefits (the 'short term attitude').
- No threat or vulnerability has materialised yet (the 'ostrich attitude'). Unfortunately many practitioners regard security as someone else's job. In many cases this leads to an undisciplined and haphazard implementation of security measures, justified by the view that 'it won't happen here'. Even at sites where serious efforts are made to manage security in a professional way, security measures are rarely designed and built into existing systems and services.
- If I spent the money involved in providing a high level of security for my IT infrastructure, some threats would still not be addressed in practice and they would be the ones to materialise (the attitude that you can't be protected from all possible threats).

A very common pitfall is a lack of senior management interest. When no threats materialize and the annual security budget increases, management tends to cut the budget rather than increase it. Part of the solution to avoid this lack of interest lies in keeping the management well informed about the IT infrastructure's level of security, by having a comprehensive security plan in which 'risks' are balanced against the measures taken. This is precisely the task of the Security Officer.

The more cumbersome the actions to be taken, the more likely they are to be evaded. As mentioned above, implementing security measures requires discipline and participation by the entire workforce. It is far easier to carry the workforce with you than to have to enforce the measures, and cheaper too!

Example

In a bank, certain employees are given access to special mainframe applications by using their common PC. They are required to sign on about 8 times using various passwords and are required to change the passwords weekly; checks are made to ensure they do not use one password for all access paths.

This is an undesirable situation. Productivity will drop, as the likelihood of people missing out or forgetting a password is very likely and they are almost forced to write down the passwords. This is a typical example of having a seemingly good security level, where the actual level is in fact low and probably dangerously low.

Another pitfall may be a gradual drop in the security level caused by not adopting the required level following changes. Making security part of the impact analysis is a good way of preventing this from happening.

Attempts to adopt every security measure that could conceivably be needed are bound to fail. In practice, a lot of attention is paid to shutting the front door, while the backdoor is left wide open.

If there is no security policy in an organisation, there is no way of telling what the desired balance is between the cost of Security Management measures and the risks covered by them. So policy is a prerequisite in working out the details of what management has to decide.

Measurements are necessary to decide what the effectiveness is of the adopted security measures. There are several pitfalls associated with measuring: the risk of data being misinterpreted or misused and the risk of privacy rights being violated.

Example

Suppose it is discovered that a particular person has asked the IT department for several password resets. What does this signify? It could be that the person concerned is inaccurate in typing his user ID and/or password, or has had several days off from the office and forgotten his password. Without other context information one would not be able to tell which applied.

New communications systems (e.g. Internet) and their applications are never designed to be secure. Why? Designing a secure system requires more effort than building an insecure system, and runs counter to the business requirement of low development costs and a short time to market. Other reasons are that designers tacitly trust the system's users to behave more or less properly, which they do not; designers do not always possess the technological skills to adequately implement security measures (often without being aware of their shortcomings); many secure systems will be supplied to customers in an insecure state. For example a lot of network products are delivered to the customer with all the security measures disabled in order to facilitate problem-free installation and operation. Also, many software products are supplied with default passwords. It is important to ensure that all of these are changed before the system becomes operational ('live').

Other pitfalls include:

■ The ambition level being too high, like:

  – Wanting to do everything at once. It is tempting to sit back and write standards or standard procedures for the entire organisation. That way, it seems, everything can be changed at once. Unfortunately for implementing information security the technical part is less significant than the organizational counterpart. And since changing organisations is more difficult than changing technique, a step-wise approach is more successful.

  – Waiting for the complete picture before introducing measures. Standards, procedures and plans are all changed regularly, after all, the world is changing continuously, so the picture is never complete.

■ Forgetting to aim for built-in safety. It is no good locking the stable door once the horse has bolted; it is better to have locks in place before the horse is brought in. That means that at the moment the stable is designed, security has to be on the agenda.

■ Lack of detection mechanisms. If you detected no faults in your database does that mean that it still has its integrity? Finding out now that a hacker has been using your system for the last six months will make you wonder at the damage that is done. Even if you cannot see any damage at this moment. Trapdoors are usually well concealed.

■ Inconsistency of the measures. Windows in a building should have the same quality locks as doors. The firewall acts as lock for people outside the internal network. But what about that internal network? How is access to crucial information protected? Hacking from inside the network, with knowledge on what information is where, and knowing what systems exist, is far easier than getting unauthorized access from the outside.

However, there are also success factors:

■ Management involvement and commitment of the board of management almost certainly guarantees success. Lack of it spells disaster. When management complies, the rest of the organisation follows.

■ Involvement of the people doing the work (having procedures drawn up by users creates support). It is very difficult to define procedures in isolation from behind the security department's desk and it also makes acceptance at floor level hard to achieve. It is more effective to use the day to day experience of users to write the instructions. After all, they are doing the job already and know how it works in detail.

■ Clear responsibility and being held accountable for it. The 'one captain rules the ship' dogma also works with managers in IT. The more people are responsible the less responsibility there is. Besides it helps when accountability issues have to be raised. Sanctions must be applied, if required, in order to have information security taken seriously.

Annex A SECURITY MANAGEMENT WITH ITIL IN RELATION TO THE CODE OF PRACTICE FOR INFORMATION SECURITY MANAGEMENT (BS7799)

BS 7799 is the definitive standard on Security Management and its recommendations should be followed when implementing Security Management. This Annex contains cross-reference information relating to this Code of Practice for Information Security Management. Table A.1 is provided to show which subjects from the Code are dealt with by ITIL. The table also shows which security-relevant subjects are not covered by ITIL because they are beyond the scope of ITIL. With regard to the latter category, a short summary is included from the Code.

The first column shows the measures from the Code of Practice for Information Security Management; the numbering is not from the Code. The second column provides either a short summary or a reference to a section of this book.

Table A.1: Elements of the Code of Practice for Information Security Management addressed by ITIL

Measures from the Code of Practice for Information Security Management	**Reference**
1. Security policy	The policy on information security is given for ITIL. The policy has to be implemented, and possibly further detailed by the IT service provider. From the ITIL point of view, the policy is 'imposed', generally by means of the SLAs.
	An idea of what is generally a good starting point for the policy on information security is given below.
	Objective To provide management support for information security. The policy should provide a clear direction. The management must demonstrate its support for the objectives.
	Summary of measures
	• The development and implementation of a policy on information security.
	• Draw up a policy document. The policy document should cover at least the following:
	– objectives and scope
	– the importance of information security for the organisation
	– general responsibilities of the management, employees and any specific responsibilities
	– the reporting of security incidents
	– general principles (e.g. the principles relating to the continuity of business processes, or the starting point that the organisational assets must not be used for private purposes).

Measures from the Code of Practice for Information Security Management	*Reference*
	• The relationships to other types of policy (e.g. the personnel policy with regard to education and periodic appraisals) as well as external requirements (e.g. statutory obligations or contracts).
	• There must also be a record of who is responsible for the security policy and how often and in what manner the policy has to be updated. The policy must be available to every employee in the organisation who is (jointly) responsible for information security.
2. Security organisation	See 4.1.1
3. Asset classification and control	See 4.2.1
3.1 Accountability for assets	Part of the ITIL Configuration and Asset Management process. See 3.3.1
4. Personnel security	See 4.2.2
5. Physical and environmental security	Some environmental issues are described in the ITIL Environmental Strategy Set and in the ITIL Environmental Management Set in the modules Accommodation Specification, Secure Power Supplies, Fire Precautions in IT Installations. Nevertheless these modules were not written from a Security Management point of view. In general, the following is good practice with regard to physical and environmental security.

Objective

To prevent unauthorised or unnecessary physical access to information and information systems; this is in order to limit the unauthorised examination, destruction or theft of information or damage to, or interference with information systems. Part of this objective is to create an environment that promotes the safe handling of information and systems.

Summary of the main measures

- **Secure areas:** accommodate IT facilities that support critical or sensitive business activities in secure areas.
- **Physical security:** define the location(s) that have to be physically secured. This may include, for instance, segmenting (compartmentalising) buildings and possibly fitted security rings. Physical security is particularly important for computer centres and rooms used for important business processes.
- **Physical access control:** protect access to secure areas or locations by means of appropriate access control, e.g. a porter, isolated access areas, a pass system or the use of access codes.
- **Import/export area for people and goods:** particularly in new buildings, it is advisable (on the basis of a risk analysis) to use an isolated area for goods delivery and collection. This considerably increases the

*Measures from
the Code of Practice
for Information
Security Management*   *Reference*

capability to controlling external threats and also reduces the number of situations in which there is a likelihood of mistakes being made by the organisation's own employees. A similar construction can be used for controlling employee and visitor access to (secured) locations.

- **Clear desk policy:** leave desks clear outside working hours and put all information away when not in use. Store sensitive information in a locked cabinet or safe. Ensure that computer equipment (PCs, terminals) is physically protected and access is protected by locks, passwords or other security measures. Also pay attention to incoming and outgoing mail points and unattended fax machines.

- **Import/export of (old) organisational assets:** have in place a procedure for bringing in and removing equipment, data and software. This also applies to the disposal of old equipment.

- **Security of equipment:** physically protect equipment. This also applies to equipment used outside an organisation's premises. Select locations or positions for installing equipment that involve the least risk from outside.

- **Power supplies:** protect the most important equipment from power failures.

- **Cabling security:** ensure cables for electricity, telephones and data communication are safely installed. Take into account the safety of people (loose cables left lying around), as well as possibilities for visual inspections (detecting tapped wires) and accessibility for maintenance.

- **Equipment maintenance:** establish procedures for maintaining equipment. Take into account subjects covered by ITIL, such as maintenance and service-contracts (Underpinning Contracts), failure records, but also the authorisation of maintenance personnel and agreements on equipment import/export, when repair work has to be done off the premises, and take precautions in connection with any information that may still be in the equipment, for example on hard disks.

6. Communications and operations management	See 4.2.3, with the following additions:
6.2.1 Capacity Planning	Is part of ITIL Performance and Capacity Management, see 3.4.3
6.2.2 System Acceptance	Is part of ITIL Change Management, see 3.3.4
6.2.3 Fallback Planning	Is part of ITIL Business Continuity Planning, see 3.4.4
6.2.4 Change Management	Is part of ITIL Change Management, see 3.3.4

*Measures from
the Code of Practice
for Information
Security Management*

	Reference
6.4 Housekeeping	ITIL does not generally go into the details of this.
6.4.1 Data Backups	Is part of ITIL Availability Management, see 3.4.2
6.4.2 Keeping a Logbook	Is part of the Incident Control/Help Desk function see 3.3.2
6.4.3 Fault Logging	Is also part of the Incident Control/Help Desk function.
6.4.4 Environmental Monitoring	Is outside the scope of ITIL.
6.7.1 Agreements concerning data exchanges	These agreements should be included in the SLA.
7. Access control	See 4.2.4 with the following additions:
7.1 Business requirement for access control	Is largely outside the scope of ITIL: The policy on access and access control: the starting points have to be laid down for access (powers and responsibilities, who's allowed to do what), authorisations (who determines who's allowed to do what), access control, and the control of these three.
7.3 User responsibilities	Is outside the scope of ITIL. This is the responsibility of the user organisation (i.e., the customer of the service provider). Encourage the user organisation to address its responsibilities more explicitly in the SLA. The framework in Annex B may be used for this purpose. The column 'H' in Table B.1 is reserved for laying down the customer's and end-user's responsibilities for security. Pay specific attention to the user responsibilities for the following topics (not exhaustive):

User responsibilities for passwords:

* Each individual user should have his own account and keep passwords secret to maintain accountability.
* Avoid keeping a paper record of passwords. When a paper record is really needed for emergency reasons, keep this paper in a sealed envelope and stored in a secure place (safe) to ensure that these passwords can only be used following the proper emergency procedures. By keeping these passwords in a sealed envelope, their usage is always noticeable, be it in a later stage.
* Change passwords at regular intervals. For average usage, it should be sufficient to change passwords every month.
* The minimum length of passwords should be six characters. Choose passwords which include numeric, alphabetic and other characters.
* Avoid using temporary passwords unless absolutely necessary but if used change them at first Login.

Measures from
the Code of Practice
for Information
Security Management   *Reference*

User responsibilities for not leaving active sessions, equipment and data carriers:

- The user should log off when leaving the equipment for some period of time.

- In any case, encourage the use of (automatic or user-initiated) screen blanking and keyboard locking.

- The user should take specific precautions when equipment, such as laptops, is used in insecure circumstances, e.g. where equipment can easily be stolen. Physical locks may be useful.

- The same applies for data carriers such as floppy disks.

User responsibilities for following import and export procedures:

- The user has a responsibility for virus-prevention and detection. End-users must check data carriers against viruses when importing them. Users should check data carriers and laptops on import for viruses and malicious software.

- Software should not be imported by the users but only through the appropriate channels, which is the Release Management process (software release and roll out).

- If users import and export, the backup-procedures cannot fully be controlled by the IT service provider. The users therefore have a responsibility, e.g. in backing up their laptop.

- Make users aware of the specific risks in teleworking situations.

User responsibilities in the use of external communications and services:

- Make users aware of the dos and don'ts on the Internet.

- The same applies to the use of electronic mail and other forms of electronic data interchange.

- Do not leave external data communication facilities open for remote access (remote access should only be possible through authorised channels).

- The user should disconnect his PC from the LAN prior to accessing the Internet. When downloading files, check for viruses. Do not use software from the Internet.

- Users should understand that facilities are provided for business purposes only.

User responsibilities in security incidents:

- Report security incidents as soon as possible through the right channel: the Incident Control/Help Desk function through which incident management takes place.

Finally, users may have a responsibility in other procedures. The above list is not exhaustive.

Measures from the Code of Practice for Information Security Management	*Reference*
8. Systems development and maintenance	Information systems development and maintenance is dealt with in the ITIL book Software Lifecycle Support and the Business Perspective Set. The following starting points are generally advisable.

Objective

To ensure that the systems offer the required level of security throughout their operational life.

Summary of measures

- Drawing up security requirements for new information systems: details of the necessary functional requirements, the security architecture and the specifications are drawn up on the basis of a thorough analysis of the needs and requirements for confidentiality, integrity and the availability of the future system. Also take into account access control, the possible segregation of duties, audit trails for verifiability, external requirements (laws, contracts), backup, system security, and ease of use. Moreover, take into account the technical security and also the aspects concerned with embedding it into the existing organisation, the necessary training, the problems of introduction and the balance with other security measures such as physical and procedural security.

- Security in application systems: besides the above measures, in application systems there is also a need for data input validation, segregation of duties in the application systems and checks to ascertain correct processing (random checks, check sums, and workflow monitoring). A risk analysis can form the basis for verifying message authenticity, authorisation and integrity (particularly in situations in which networks are used involving third parties) and encryption may be used.

- The testing, acceptance, introduction and security of new and old system resources (part of Change Management): depending on the size of the operation, the installation of new systems may call for an instruction handbook in which the current production is considered, the system being replaced stays on stand-by for as long as possible and clear go/no-go points are included. Ensure there is a proper test plan. As far as possible, separate the test/acceptance environment from the operational environment. Do not carry out tests directly on the operational data but on copies and, if confidentiality or privacy plays a role, on simulated data (fake input). Save the test details for possible later analysis. Also ensure there is a proper acceptance procedure. Check and manage changes in operational software; consider the updating of program libraries and fitting patches in existing software.

- Security in development and support environments: draw up procedures for the system development activities. It is advisable to follow a formal development method. This reduces the likelihood of errors or unintentional differences between the various development phases and makes development activities more controllable.

Measures from the Code of Practice for Information Security Management	Reference
	• Changes in the operating system: analyse the possible consequences of changes to security and applications, for example. Draw up a test plan and document its implementation.
	• Changes to software packages: as far as possible, the organisation should avoid making its own changes to standard software packages. If changes are deemed essential, carefully examine the consequences for the package's continuity (consider the implications for new versions) and work out a strategy with the supplier.
8.1 Security requirements of systems	See 4.2
9. Business Continuity Management	Continuity planning is part of the ITIL Business Continuity Planning process, which is described in a separate ITIL book, see Contingency/Planning. A brief overview is given below. Objective To make continuity plans to deal with major unforeseeable failures or disasters, as well as the continuation of critical business processes. Summary of measures The process of continuity planning: Put in place procedures for developing, maintaining and updating continuity plans throughout the organisation, beginning with the most critical business processes. Ensure there is a consistent structure in place for continuity planning throughout the organisation. Co-ordination is essential in drawing up the plans. Continuity planning should cover at least the following: • Procedures for emergency situations: a description of the responsibilities and the activities that have to be carried out immediately in the event of a disaster. • Fallback procedures: a description of the activities that have to be carried out to enable critical business processes to continue, possibly in an alternative manner, or to enable processes to be restored as quickly as possible, possibly at another location. • Follow-up procedures: the activities that restore the original situation and the normal business operations. • Test schedules: Test continuity plans regularly, at least annually, and every time major changes are made and carry out exercises.
10. Compliance	See also 4.3
10.1 Compliance with legal requirements	Compliance with legal or statutory and contractual requirements is not a specific subject of ITIL, although it is obviously relevant to the IT service provider. Give the following points special attention:

**Measures from
the Code of Practice
for Information
Security Management**   **Reference**

Objective

To check compliance with the organisation's security policy and the applicable standards, and also to prevent breaches of statutory or contractual security requirements.

Summary of measures

- Copyright protection: supervision to prevent illegal copying or use of software or other copyrighted material. Issue personnel with guidelines. A procedure is required for the import and export of data carriers, and make regular audits of the software in use and compare these with the list of 'legal' software. This should take into account both third party copyrighted material and the organisation's own material.

- Organisational documents: protect the most important documents of an organisation from loss, destruction and falsification. The (statutory) periods for which records have to be securely retained must also be taken into account. Information must also be accessible within a reasonable time. This places high requirements on the availability of the (old) information systems and readers for old data carriers, or the timely conversion to new versions. For example, consider the timely conversion from the large $5\frac{1}{4}$ inch floppy disks to the small $3\frac{1}{2}$ inch format.

- Personal data: legislation on personal information records must be respected. The Data Protection Registrar has issued advice containing details of the expected measures.

Annex B SPECIMEN SECURITY SECTION IN THE SLA

As far as possible, specify security requirements in the SLA in measurable terms. An SLA is a formal contract between the organisation and an IT service provider. The security section should ensure that the organisation's security requirements and standards are fulfilled in a *verifiable* way. The SLA is signed by both parties.

Subjects which require attention in the SLA's security section include:

- The general policy on information security.
- The permitted methods of access and the management and use of user identification (IDs) and passwords.
- The IT service provider's obligation to keep a list of authorised persons.
- Agreements about auditing and logging.
- The obligation to record management activities that are relevant to security.
- The times and days on which the service is available (if necessary, take fallback facilities into account)
- The obligations of each party (in terms of what the responsibilities of the organisation and the IT service provider are).
- Procedures for protecting organisational assets (including information).
- Responsibilities for legal matters (e.g. the Data Protection Act).
- The right to supervise the activities of users (and the right to revoke this right).
- Responsibilities for installing and maintaining equipment and software.
- The right to check contractual responsibilities.
- Restrictions on copying information and making it public.
- Measures intended to ensure that information and goods are destroyed or returned upon the contract's termination.
- Any physical security measures that are required.
- The management process for information security at the IT service providers.
- Procedures to ensure adherence to security measures.
- Training for users on methods, procedures and security.
- Measures intended to ensure computer viruses cannot be spread.

- An authorisation procedure for user access rights.
- Agreements on reporting and investigating security incidents. Contact persons for urgent security incidents in the organisation (e.g. the Security Officer) and at the IT service provider's (e.g. the Security Manager).
- Taking security measures that comply with the baseline and additional measures for information with a higher classification.

Table B.1 is provided as an example and can be included in a general Service Level Agreement. The table is intended to provide an overview of the security measures required by the customer and the realisation of those requirements by the IT service provider.

Column B summarises the main subject from the Code of Practice for Information Security Management. The customer can indicate in column C which of these measures are expected, and to what degree. The IT service provider can indicate in columns D and E which measures are provided as part of the standard service and which measures are provided at an extra charge. If required, column E can be used to distinguish the specific measures for the various levels of classification. Sometimes more than one party is involved in providing a service and security measures apply to all of them. In those cases, columns F and G can be used to refer to the relevant contracts.

The customer also has to take measures to achieve a clear security policy. Columns H and I can be used to indicate the organisation's officers responsible for compliance with the measures on the part of the customer as well as the IT service provider.

Table B.1: Security requirements and solutions

A	B	C	D	E
		Customer	Service Catalogue	
		Service Level Requirements: the customer's need for security	The standard level of security offered by the IT service provider	These are the Additional security arrangements
No.	Code of Practice for Information Security Management	Security requirements	Security baseline	Additional security
I	Security policy			
I.I	Security Policy			
2	Security Organisation			
2.I	Information security infrastructure			
2.2	Security of third party access			
3	Asset clarification and control			

It is important to check all the measures, on the one hand because the customer may be held responsible in the event of the IT service provider's default, and, on the other hand, to obtain an insight into the effectiveness of the measures, so that they can be tightened or possibly relaxed, if necessary.

Various types of checks are possible. One possibility is a desk study based on reports and security incidents; another possibility is regular audits by an external party to check that the IT service provider is implementing the security measures.

Reports on the planned and implemented security measures are important for checking progress and status. Reports on security incidents are necessary to be able to verify the effectiveness of the measures. Additional agreements with the Incident Control/Help Desk are necessary for recognising and dealing with security incidents. These agreements have to be drawn up in consultation with the IT service provider and the customer (since in many cases the end user, being employees of the customer, are involved in some way with security incidents; e.g. they create them, or they detect them). Security incidents that result in the immediate involvement of a Security Officer or other parties require specific attention.

The entire range of security measures is laid down at the time of establishing the security plan (see Annex C). As the measures will need to be changed, it is advisable to have an appropriate procedure, so that changes to security measures can be checked here too. The existing procedures in the Change Management process can be used for this.

F	G	H	I	J
Services from third parties	Implementation	Division of responsibilities		
Reference to Underpinning Contracts	More detailed description	regarding the implementation, management and control of the measures	regarding the implementation, management and control of the measures	regarding the implementation, management and control of the measures
Reference	*Description*	*Customer*	*Provider A*	*Provider B*

A	B	C	D	E
		Customer	Service Catalogue	
		Service Level Requirements: the customer's need for security	The standard level of security offered by the IT service provider	These are the Additional security arrangements
No.	Code of Practice for Information Security Management	Security requirements	Security baseline	Additional security
3.1	Accountability for assets			
3.2	Information classification			
4	Personnel security			
4.1	Security in job definition and resourcing			
4.2	User training			
4.3	Responding to security incidents			
5	Physical and environmental security			
5.1	Secure areas			
5.2	Equipment security			
6	Communications and operations management			
6.1	Operational procedures and responsibilities			
6.2	System planning and acceptance			
6.3	Protection from malicious software			
6.4	Housekeeping			
6.5	Network management			
6.6	Media handling and security			
6.7	Data and software exchange			

F	G	H	I	J
Services from third parties	Implementation	Division of responsibilities		
Reference to Underpinning Contracts	More detailed description	regarding the implementation, management and control of the measures	regarding the implementation, management and control of the measures	regarding the implementation, management and control of the measures
Reference	*Description*	*Customer*	*Provider A*	*Provider B*

A	B	C	D	E
		Customer	Service Catalogue	
		Service Level Requirements: the customer's need for security	The standard level of security offered by the IT service provider	These are the Additional security arrangements
No.	Code of Practice for Information Security Management	Security requirements	Security baseline	Additional security
7	Access control			
7.1	Business requirement for control/access			
7.2	User access management			
7.3	User responsibilities			
7.4	Network access control			
7.5	Computer access control			
7.6	Application access control			
7.7	Monitoring system access and use			
8	Systems development and maintenance			
8.1	Security requirements of systems			
8.2	Security in application systems			
8.3	Security of application system files			
8.4	Security in development and support environments			
9	Business continuity management			
9.1	Aspects of business continuity planning			
10	Compliance			
10.1	Compliance with legal requirements			

F	G	H	I	J
Services from third parties	Implementation	Division of responsibilities		
Reference to Underpinning Contracts	More detailed description	regarding the implementation, management and control of the measures	regarding the implementation, management and control of the measures	regarding the implementation, management and control of the measures
Reference	*Description*	*Customer*	*Provider A*	*Provider B*

A	B	C	D	E
		Customer	Service Catalogue	
		Service Level Requirements: the customer's need for security	The standard level of security offered by the IT service provider	These are the Additional security arrangements
No.	**Code of Practice for Information Security Management**	**Security requirements**	**Security baseline**	**Additional security**
10.2	Security reviews of IT systems			
10.3	System audit considerations			

F	G	H	I	J
Services from third parties	Implementation	Division of responsibilities		
Reference to Underpinning Contracts	More detailed description	regarding the implementation, management and control of the measures	regarding the implementation, management and control of the measures	regarding the implementation, management and control of the measures
Reference	*Description*	*Customer*	*Provider A*	*Provider B*

Annex C FRAMEWORK FOR DRAWING UP A SECURITY PLAN

As information security begins with an abstract policy and ends in specific measures, it is worthwhile drawing up a plan in which everything is clear and verifiable. As taking the measures costs money, the plan should also contain some form of financial reporting and accounting.

ITIL is a set of structured best practices. This section therefore describes an approach that can be used in practice. One or more SLAs form the starting point for drawing up the security plan, and possibly also the information security policy (policy guidelines). The IT service provider draws up his own security plan, which customers will generally want to examine or have examined, in connection with regular EDP audits and other accounting information.

The security plan is intended to clearly allocate the responsibility for fulfilling the obligations that arise from the SLAs to various departments and/or individuals. These internal arrangements are nothing more than *Operational Level Agreements*. This is illustrated in the table below. Only a small part is shown below. The table is derived from the SLA and the arrangements in the baseline. Columns A and B again show all the measures taken from, for example, the Code of Practice for Information Security Management. Column C shows the agreements with the customer and columns D and E show the remaining obligations (see Annex B for further details). These obligations are clearly allocated to the organisation's officers and departments in the next columns.

Table C.1: A security plan

A	B	C	D	E	H	I	J
		Customer	Service Catalogue		Operational Level Agreements: Division of responsibilities in the IT service provider's organisation		
					regarding the implementation, management and control of the measures	regarding the implementation, management and control of the measures	regarding the implementation, management and control of the measures
No.	*Code of Practice for Information Security Management*	*Security requirements*	*Security baseline*	*Additional security*	*Officer O*	*Department A*	*Department B*
		Measures group x					
		Security measure xyz					
		Measures group y					
		A security measure					
		Another security measure					
		Get the picture?					

C.1   Working with profiles

The advantage of the above approach is its convenience. As will become clear, the disadvantage is the need to maintain it. After all, a change in agreements about the management of user rights on the part of the IT service provider, for example, will affect many departments.

It may therefore be worthwhile defining profiles. A profile is a set of measures that are often found together, e.g. the measures for certain IT components or certain user groups. This grouping of measures helps to ease the maintenance of the management system. The following profiles have proven useful in practice:

- profile 'all employees': the measures that all the employees, either in the organisation of the customer (the end user) or in the organisation of the IT service provider, have to implement

- profile 'personnel': all the measures concerned with taking on, training, ongoing training, and employment termination (voluntary or otherwise)

- profile 'organisation': the measures that collectively form the management framework

Annex D LITERATURE

The following literature was used in compiling this book and/or is recommended to readers who would like to gain a better understanding of information security and management.

Dennis Bladergroen et al, *Planning en beheersing van IT-dienstverlening*, ISBN 90-267-2156-0, 1995

A Code of Practice for Information Security Management, BS 7799: 1995

A Code of Practice for Information Security Management, BS 7799: 1999 Draft

Code voor Informatiebeveiliging – een leidraad voor beleid en implementatie, NNI, 1994

Sander Koppens en Bas Meijberg, *Operationeel beheer Informatiesystemen*, ISBN 90-267-1841-1

Edo Roos Lindgreen, *A Sense of Secureness*, ISBN 90 900 9320 6, 1996

Maarten Looijen, *IT bedreigd*, ISBN 90 267 2500 0, 1996

Arnold van Marmeren et al, *Understanding and Improving your IT Infrastructure*, ISBN 0113306792

Paul L. Overbeek, *Towards secure open systems*, ISBN 90-9005824-9, 2nd edition, July 1993

Visie op informatiebeveiliging, ISBN 90-803102-3-9, 1996

Informatiebeveiliging in de praktijk, ISBN 90-803102-2-0, 1996

D.1 Further reading

Detailed guidance on the individual IT Service Management functions can be found in the individual ITIL books within the *Service Support, Service Delivery and Managers* sets, including:

Configuration Management, ISBN 0113305303

Help Desk, ISBN 0113305222

Problem Management, ISBN 0113305273

Change Management, ISBN 0113305257

Software Control & Distribution, ISBN 0113305370

Availability Management, ISBN 0113305516

Capacity Management, ISBN 0113305443

Contingency Planning, ISBN 0113305249

Cost Management for IT Services, ISBN 0113305478

Service Level Management-Customer Focused, ISBN 0113305214

Customer Liaison, ISBN 011330546X

IT Services Organisation, ISBN 011330563X

Managing Facilities Management, ISBN 0113305265

Planning and Control for IT Services, ISBN 0113305486

Quality Management for IT services, ISBN 0113305559

Code of Practice for IT Service Management, ISBN 0580295826

D.2 Useful contacts

This book is part of the IT Infrastructure Library (ITIL). ITIL is managed by the Central Computer and Telecommunications Agency (CCTA), which is an executive agency of the UK Office of Public Service. The address is:

CCTA, Rosebery Court, St Andrews Business Park, Norwich, NR7 0HS, United Kingdom.

While the information in this book gives an idea of the benefits possible from an ITIL approach, it does not, of course, answer all the questions. We would advise the reader to meet and talk with others in a similar position, or those who have already done what you are setting out to do. Helpful contacts and the chance to discuss appropriate topics are offered by the itSMF. Established as the user group for ITIL, they offer their members an invaluable forum for professionals, including seminars on relevant topics and an annual conference. Contact addresses are:

for Benelux: itSMF Netherlands, PO Box 1260 BB Zeewolde, the Netherlands

for UK and elsewhere: itSMF, 1A Taverners Square, Silver Road, Norwich NR3 4SY, UK.

D.3 Information and help

The following organisations provide information and/or help on the subject of information security.

Organisation	URL
Australian Defense Signals Directorate: many security links, policy papers and more (AU)	http://www.dsd.gov.au
Bundesamt für Sicherheit in der Informationstechnik: German information security handbooks, articles and more (DE)	http://www.bsi.bund.de
Singapore Computer Emergency Response Team – Security information and advisories (SG)	http://www.singcert.org.sg
National Computing Centre Ltd: information security services (UK)	http://www.ncc.co.uk
Centre for Secure Information Systems @ George Mason University (US)	http://www.isse.gmu.edu/~csis/
International Computer Security Association (previously NCSA) (US)	http://www.icsa.net

National Security Agency (US)	http://www.nsa.gov:8080
OpenBSDUNIX security (US)	http://www.openbsd.org/security
JAVA security frequently asked questions (US)	http://www.sun.com/sfaq
Computer Emergency Response Team – Security information and advisories (US)	http://www.cert.org
Forum of Incident and Security Teams and pointers to other information security related sources (US)	http://www.first.org_

Annex E GLOSSARY OF TERMS

E.1   Acronyms and abbreviations used in this Module:

BSI
> British Standards Institute

CCTA
> Central Computer and Telecommunications Agency

CI
> Configuration Item

CoP
> Code of Practice

CRAMM
> CCTA Risk Analysis and Management Methodology

EDP
> Electronic Data Processing

ICT
> Information and Communication Technology

ISO
> International Standards Organisation

IT
> Information Technology

ITIL
> Information Technology Infrastructure Library, a trademark of CCTA

KPI
> Key Performance Indicator

LAN
> Local Area Network

OLA
> Operational Level Agreement

RFC
> Request for Change

SLA
> Service Level Agreement

SLR
> Service Level Requirements

E.2 Definitions

Availability

the ability of a component or a service to perform its required function at a stated instant or over a stated period of time

Baseline Security

the security level adopted by the IT organisation for its own security and from the point of view of good 'due diligence'

Configuration Item (CI)

a component of an infrastructure – or an item, such as a request for change, associated with an infrastructure – which is (or is to be) under the control of Configuration and Asset Management. CIs may vary widely in complexity, size and type – from an entire system (including all hardware, software and documentation) to a single module or a minor hardware component

Customer

recipient of the service; usually the customer management has responsibility for the cost of the service, either directly through charging or indirectly in terms of demonstrable business need

Incident Control/Help Desk

a single point of contact with the service enterprise for end-users of services. This functional group is often referred to as a service desk. Its core process is normally incident management

Impact

a measure of the scale and magnitude of an incident or problem

Incident

any event which is not part of the standard operation of a system. It will have an impact on the system, although this may be slight and may be even transparent to users

Incident Control

the process of identifying, recording, classifying and progressing incidents until affected services return to normal operation

IT Infrastructure

the sum of an organisation's IT related hardware, software, data telecommunication facilities, procedures and documentation

IT service

a described set of facilities, IT and non-IT, supported by the IT service provider that fulfils one or more needs of the customer and that is perceived by the customer as a coherent whole

IT service provider

the role of IT service provider is performed by any organisational units, whether internal or external, that deliver and support IT services to a customer

Key Performance Indicator

the measurable quantities against which specific performance criteria can be set when drawing up the SLA

Known Error

> a condition identified by successful diagnosis of the root cause of a problem when it is confirmed that a CI is at fault

Operational Level Agreements

> internal agreements covering the delivery of services which support the services enterprise in their delivery of services

Performance Criteria

> the expected levels of achievement which are set within the SLA against specific Key Performance Indicators

Problem

> unknown underlying cause of one or more incidents

Process

> a series of actions or operations designed to achieve an end

Security Management

> the process of managing a defined level of security on information and services

Security Manager

> the Security Manager is the role that is responsible for the Security Management process in the service provider organisation. The person is responsible for fulfilling the security demands as specified in the SLA, either directly or through delegation by the Service Level Manager. The Security Officer and the Security Manager work closely together

Security Officer

> the Security Officer is responsible for assessing the business risks and setting the security policy. As such, this role is the counterpart of the Security Manager and resides in the customer's business organisation. The Security Officer and the Security Manager work closely together

Segregation of duties

> separation of the management or execution of certain duties or of areas of responsibility is required in order to prevent and reduce opportunities for unauthorised modification or misuse of data or service

Service Level

> the expression of an aspect of a service in definitive and quantifiable terms

Service Level Agreement

> a formal agreement between the customer(s) and the IT service provider specifying service levels and the terms under which a service or a package of services is provided to the customer(s)

Best Practice:
the OGC approach with ITIL® and PRINCE®

OGC Best Practice is an approach to management challenges as well as the application of techniques and actions.

Practical, flexible and adaptable, management guidance from OGC translates the very best of the world's practices into guidance of an internationally recognised standard. Both PRINCE2 and ITIL publications can help every organisation to:

- Run projects more efficiently
- Reduce project risk
- Purchase IT more cost effectively
- Improve organisational Service Delivery.

What is ITIL and why use it?

ITIL's starting point is that organisations do not simply use IT; they depend on it. Managing IT as effectively as possible must therefore be a high priority.

ITIL consists of a unique library of guidance on providing quality IT services. It focuses tightly on the customer, cost effectiveness and building a culture that puts the emphasis on IT performance.

Used by hundreds of the world's most successful organisations, its core titles are available in print, Online Subscription and CD-ROM formats. They are:

- Service Support
- Service Delivery
- Planning to Implement Service Management
- Application Management
- ICT Infrastructure Management
- Security Management
- The Business Perspective Volume 1 and 2
- Software Asset Management

What is PRINCE2 and why use it?

Since its introduction in 1989, PRINCE has been widely adopted by both the public and private sectors and is now recognised as a de facto standard for project management – and for the management of change.

PRINCE2, the most evolved version, is driven by its experts and users to offer control, transparency, focus and ultimate success for any project you need to implement.

Publications are available in various formats: print, Online Subscription and CD-ROM. Its main titles are:

- Managing Successful Projects with PRINCE2
- People Issues and PRINCE2
- PRINCE2 Pocket Book
- Tailoring PRINCE2
- Business Benefits through Project Management

Other related titles:
- Passing the PRINCE2 Examinations
- Managing Successful Programmes
- Management of Risk – Guidance for Practitioners
- Buying Software – A best practice approach

Ordering

The full range of ITIL and PRINCE2 publications can be purchased direct via **www.get-best-practice.co.uk** or through calling TSO Customer Services on **0870 600 5522**. If you are outside of the UK please contact your local agent, for details email **sales@tso.co.uk** For information on Network Licenses for CD-ROM and Online Subscription please email **network.sales@tso.co.uk**

You are also able to subscribe to content online through this website or by calling TSO Customer Services on **0870 600 5522**. For more information on how to subscribe online please refer to our help pages on the website.

Other Information Sources and Services

The IT Service Management Forum (itSMF)

The IT Service Management Forum Ltd (itSMF) is the only internationally recognised and independent body dedicated to IT Service Management. It is a not-for-profit organisation, wholly owned, and principally operated, by its membership.

The itSMF is a major influence on, and contributor to, Industry Best Practice and Standards worldwide, working in partnership with OGC (the owners of ITIL), the British Standards Institution (BSI), the Information Systems Examination Board (ISEB) and the Examination Institute of the Netherlands (EXIN).

Founded in the UK in 1991, there are now a number of chapters around the world with new ones seeking to join all the time. There are well in excess of 1000 organisations covering over 10,000 individuals represented in the membership. Organisations range from large multi-nationals such as AXA, GuinnessUDV, HP, Microsoft and Procter & Gamble in all market sectors, through central & local bodies, to independent consultants.

How to contact us:

The IT Service Management Forum Ltd
Webbs Court
8 Holmes Road
Earley
Reading RG6 7BH
Tel: +44 (0) 118 926 0888
Fax: +44 (0) 118 926 3073
Email: service@itsmf.com
or visit our web-site at:
www.itsmf.com

ITIL training and professional qualifications

There are currently two examining bodies offering equivalent qualifications: ISEB (The Information Systems Examining Board), part of the British Computer Society, and Stitching EXIN (The Netherlands Examinations Institute). Jointly with OGC and itSMF (the IT Service Management Forum), they work to ensure that a common standard is adopted for qualifications worldwide. The syllabus is based on the core elements of ITIL and complies with ISO9001 Quality Standard. Both ISEB and EXIN also accredit training organisations to deliver programmes leading to qualifications.

For further information:

visit ISEB's web-site at:
www.bcs.org.uk

and EXIN:
www.exin.nl

Dear customer ■ ■ ■ ■ ■ ■ ■ ■ ■ ■ ■ ■ ■ ■ ■

We would like to hear from you with any comments or suggestions that you have on how we can improve our current products or develop new ones for the ITIL series. Please complete this questionnaire and we will enter you into our quarterly draw. The winner will receive a copy of Software Asset Management worth £35!

1 Personal Details

Name ....

Organisation ....

Job Title ....

Department ....

Address ....

....

Postcode ....

Telephone Number ....

Email ....

2 Nature of Organisation (tick one box only)

☐ Consultancy/Training
☐ Computing/IT/Software
☐ Industrial
☐ Central Government
☐ Local Government
☐ Academic/Further education
☐ Private Health
☐ Public Health (NHS)
☐ Finance
☐ Construction
☐ Telecommunications
☐ Utilities
☐ Other (Please specify)

....

3 How did you hear about ITIL?

☐ Work/Colleagues
☐ Internet/Web (please specify)

....

☐ Marketing Literature
☐ itSMF
☐ Other (please specify)

....

4 Where did you purchase this book?

☐ Web – www.tso.co.uk/bookshop
☐ Web – www.get-best-practice.co.uk
☐ Web – Other (please specify)

....

☐ Bookshop (please specify)

....

☐ Training Course
☐ Other (please specify)

....

5 How many people use ITIL in your company?

☐ 1-5
☐ 6-10
☐ 11-50
☐ 51-200
☐ 201+

6 How many people use your copy of this title?

☐ 0
☐ 1-5
☐ 6-10
☐ 11+

7 Overall, how do you rate this title?

☐ Excellent
☐ Very Good
☐ Good
☐ Fair
☐ Poor

8 What do you most like about the book? (tick all that apply)

☐ Ease of use
☐ Well structured
☐ Contents
☐ Index
☐ Hints and tips
☐ Other (Please specify)

....

9 Do you have any suggestions for improvement?

....

....

....

....

10 How do you use this book? (tick all that apply)

☐ Problem Solver
☐ Reference
☐ Tutorial
☐ Other (please specify)

....

[PTO]

11 Did you know there are 7 core titles in the **ITIL** series?

☐ No
☐ Yes

12 Do you have any other **ITIL** titles?

☐ No
☐ Yes (please specify)

....

13 Do you use the **ITIL** CDs?

☐ No
☐ Yes (please specify)

....

14 Are you aware that most of the **ITIL** series is now available as online content at **www.get-best-practice.co.uk?**

☐ Yes
☐ No

15 Do you currently subscribe to any online content found at **www.get-best-practice.co.uk?**

☐ No
☐ Yes (please specify)

....

16 Did you know that you can network your CDs and Online Subscription, to offer your project managers access to this material at their desktop?

Yes/No

☐ Please tick this box if you require further information.

17 Did you know that you are able to purchase a maintenance agreement for your CD-ROM that will allow you to receive immediately any revised versions, at no additional cost?

Yes/No

☐ Please tick this box if you require further information.

18 What business change guidance/methods does your company use?

☐ PRINCE2
☐ Managing Successful Programmes
☐ Management of Risk
☐ Successful Delivery Toolkit
☐ Business Systems Development (BSD)
☐ Other (please specify)

....

19 What is the job title of the person who makes the decision to implement **ITIL** and/or purchase IT?

....

....

20 Which three websites do you visit the most?

1 ....

2 ....

3 ....

21 Which 3 professional magazines do you read the most?

1 ....

2 ....

3 ....

22 Will you be attending any events or conferences this year related to IT, if so, which?

....

To enter your Questionnaire into our monthly draw please return this form to our Freepost Address:

**Marketing – ITIL Questionnaire
TSO
Freepost ANG4748
Norwich
NR3 1YX**

The ITIL series is available in a range of formats: hard copy, CD-ROM and now available as an Online Subscription. For further details and to purchase visit **www.get-best-practice.co.uk**

Any further enquiries or questions about ITIL or the Office of Government Commerce should be directed to the OGC Service Desk:

The OGC Service Desk
Rosebery Court
St Andrews Business Park
Norwich
NR7 0HS

Email: ServiceDesk@ogc.gsi.gov.uk
Telephone: 0845 000 4999

TSO will not sell, rent or pass any of your details onto interested third parties. The details you supply will be used for market research purposes only and to keep you up to date with TSO products and services which we feel maybe of interest to you. **If you would like us to use your information to keep you updated please indicate how you would like us to communicate with you:**

Telephone ☐   Email ☐   Mail ☐